THE TRAINS OF SERENDIB

—A Rail Journey Through Sri Lanka—

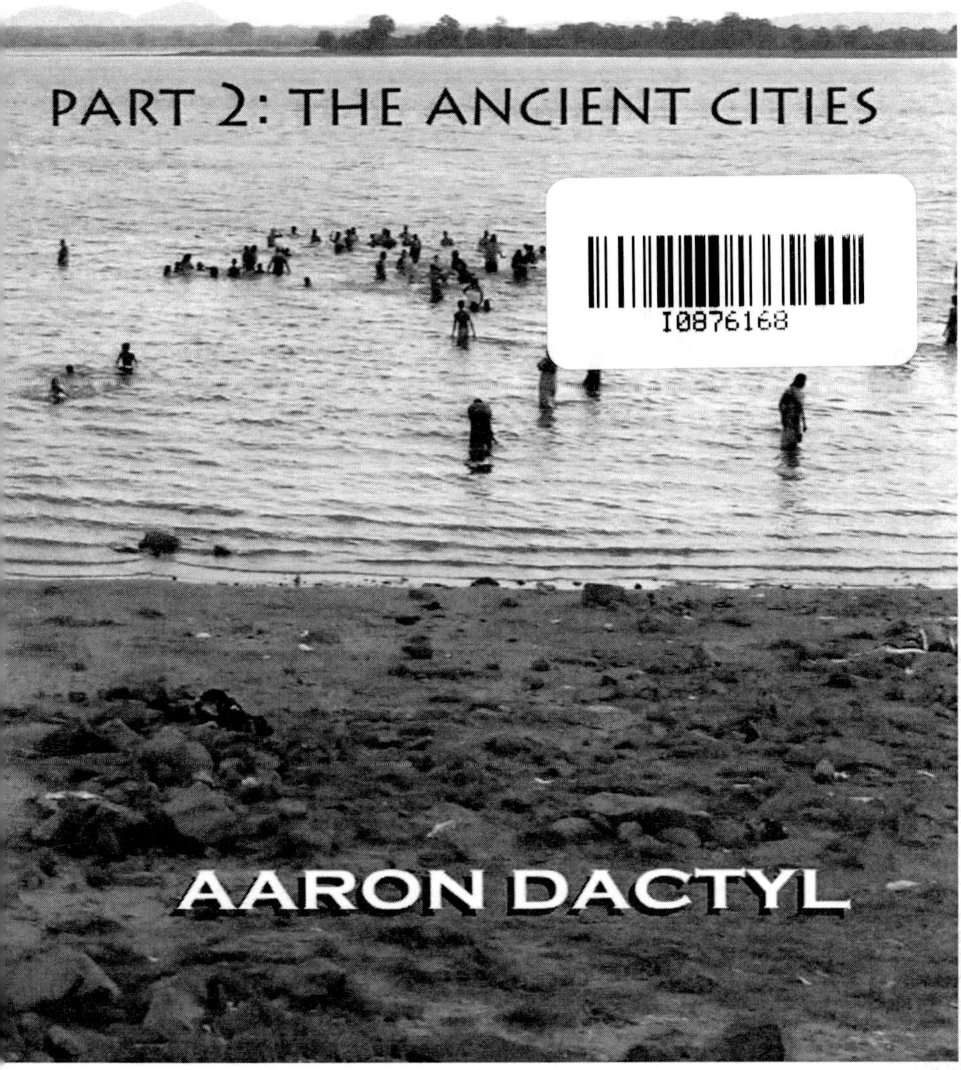

PART 2: THE ANCIENT CITIES

AARON DACTYL

OHS Press
BINFORD & MORT
WSU PRESS
THE SINDBAD VOYAGE TIM SEVERIN
ARENA
Christopher Ondaatje
THE MAN-EATER OF PUNA
SRI LANKA: THE COOKBOOK
PRAKASH K SIVANATHAN
NIRANJALA M ELLAWALA
TUTTLE
July, 1948
THE NATIONAL GEOGRAPHIC MAGAZINE
Vol. XCIV, No. 1
NATIONAL GEOGRAPHIC JANUARY 1979
LOS ANGELES ABRIGO DO SOL DIAMONDS BISON KILL SRI LANKA
NATIONAL GEOGRAPHIC NOVEMBER 2016
alphabet cooking
S is for sri lankan
ADELE BARKER
NOT QUITE PARADISE
AN AMERICAN SOJOURN IN SRI LANKA
BEACON
Henry W. Cave
Ceylon along the Rail Track
AN ACCOUNT of the INTERIOR OF CEYLON
CEYLON HISTORICAL JOURNAL
SRI LANKA BY RAIL
Royston Ellis
Globe Pequot
Bradt
The Viceroy Special
Hemasiri Fernando
Tea Time with Terrorists
Meadows
Soft Skull Press
WOOLF
THE VILLAGE IN THE JUNGLE
WOOLF
THE VILLAGE IN THE JUNGLE
OXFORD

Trains of Serendib: A Rail Journey Through Sri Lanka
Part Two: The Ancient Cities

ISBN 9781621068976

This is Microcosm #649

For a catalog, write or visit:

Microcosm Publishing

2752 N Williams Ave.

Portland, OR 97227

www.Microcosm.Pub

To join the ranks of high-class stores that feature Microcosm titles, talk to your rep: In the U.S. **Como** (Atlantic), **Fujii** (Midwest), **Book Travelers West** (Pacific), **Turnaround** in Europe, **Manda/UTP** in Canada, **New South** in Australia, and **GPS** in Asia, India, Africa, and South America.We are sold in the gift market by **Gifts of Nature.**

Did you know that you can buy our books directly from us at sliding scale rates? Support a small, independent publisher and pay less than Amazon's price at www.**Microcosm.Pub**

Global labor conditions are bad, and our roots in industrial Cleveland in the 70s and 80s made us appreciate the need to treat workers right. Therefore, our books are MADE IN THE USA and printed on post-consumer paper.

Microcosm Publishing is Portland's most diversified publishing house and distributor with a focus on the colorful, authentic, and empowering. Our books and zines have put your power in your hands since 1996, equipping readers to make positive changes in their lives and in the world around them. Microcosm emphasizes skill-building, showing hidden histories, and fostering creativity through challenging conventional publishing wisdom with books and bookettes about DIY skills, food, bicycling, gender, self-care, and social justice. What was once a distro and record label was started by Joe Biel in his bedroom and has become among the oldest independent publishing houses in Portland, OR. We are a politically moderate, centrist publisher in a world that has inched to the right for the past 80 years.

THE TRAINS OF SERENDIB

-A RAIL JOURNEY THROUGH SRI LANKA-

PART 2: THE ANCIENT CITIES

Aaron Dactyl

 All travels took place during the late summer/fall of 2013.

First Edition, First Printing

This is Part 2 of a three-part series. Parts 1 and 3 have been or will be released seperately. If you represent a literary agency or publisher and would like to see this book as a whole, bound in published form, please feel free to contact the author at:
theformer@hotmail.com

Library of Congress Cataloging-in-Publications Data

Dactyl, Aaron.
The Trains of Serendib: A Rail Journey Through Sri Lanka, Part 2
travel-prose / Aaron Dactyl. –1st Ed.
p. cm.
ISBN 0-316-92004-5 (pb)
I. Title
PS3573.A425635154 2019
813'.54 – dc20 14-3062

10 9 8 7 6 5 4 3 2 1

OR

Anna Livia Plurabella Publishing

Printed in the United States of America

5. Main Line

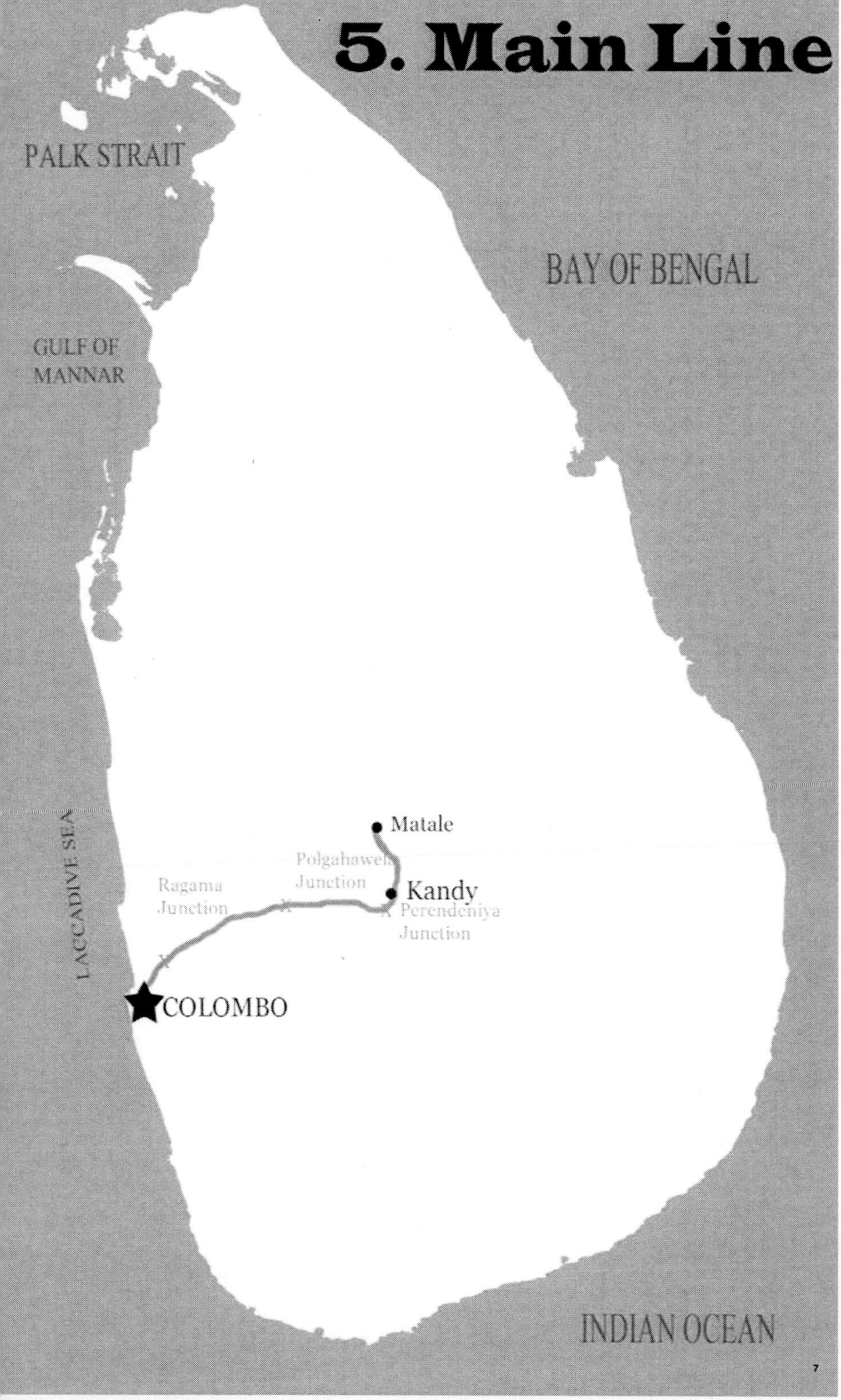
PALK STRAIT
BAY OF BENGAL
GULF OF MANNAR
LACCADIVE SEA
Matale
Polgahawela Junction
Ragama Junction
Kandy
Perendeniya Junction
COLOMBO
INDIAN OCEAN

No train line on the island displays the full scope of Sri Lanka's grandeur as concisely as the Main Line, from Colombo to Kandy, the oldest rails on the island.

When the British took control of the island — then known as Ceylon — in the early 1800s, the untamed nature of the land rendered traveling just about anywhere outside Colombo a tedious and taxing affair. The interior of the island in particular — dense mountainous jungle — posed an array of daunting physical barriers to the extent that few from the hill country had ever laid eyes on the vast ocean surrounding them. To reach the then Sinhalese capital Kandy one had to travel on foot along a succession of steep, narrow trails through the jungle over the course of a week, vulnerable to all variation of endangerment. During the rainy season this trek could take up to six weeks. It's no wonder then that both the Portuguese and Dutch failed repeatedly to control Kandy (although the Portuguese did manage to burn the city to the ground several times). Not until 1815 did Kandy finally capitulate, and it did so mainly because the Kandyan chiefs, in uncharacteristic revolt, sided with the British in disposing of their own king. That, and the reality that the Mahaweli Ganga had finally been bridged.

The main impetus for improving travel between Colombo and Kandy was, at first, purely economic: coffee and tea were flourishing in the upcountry but much difficulty persisted in transporting these commodities to port. To address this the British first constructed a road to Kandy, a 72-mile gravel affair that within a year was open to common traffic. This gave birth to the Kandy Mail Coach — the first mail coach in all of Asia. Following this success the British went on a bit of an engineering binge, constructing roads to a number of hard-to-reach districts, including the upcountry. However, due to the difficulties inherent in maintaining these thoroughfares in the face of natural erosion, only the road to Kandy remained in shape for year-round travel. Yet still, travel by carriage remained a two-day journey at best. The railway would alter this forever.

The genesis of a national railway bubbled to life in 1845 with the formation of the Ceylon Railway Company and the official surveying of possible routes to link Colombo to Kandy. Yet another decade would pass before a contract was signed with the government and more serious planning got underway. And although ground was officially broken in 1858, construction did not being in earnest until 1864. Yet by December of that first year the train made its inaugural run from Colombo and Ambepussa, covering 34 miles of track. Regular passenger service began in October of the next year, and a little more than a year after that trains had reached Polgahawela, ten miles further. The real grind lay ahead.

By 1866 construction had all but come to a halt due to the intense tunneling and grading required to penetrate the hill country. The next twenty miles of track proceeded at a literal crawl as workers tunneled through cliff after sheer cliff, manually cutting through heavy rock space enough to pass a full-time train. After supply trains first began venturing up the incline in March, 1867, two bridges — one spanning the Nanu

Oya and one over the Mahaweli Ganga — had to be constructed before the train could make its maiden voyage to Kandy, a journey that just a year before seemed far-fetched if not impossible. The dawn of April 26th, 1867, saw the first train arriving in Kandy; for many it was the ushering in of a new era.

*

The Main Line can essentially be divided into two sections — Lowlands and Highlands — each of which can further be divided ten segments — ten total. The Lowlands section — the first six segments of track, totaling forty-five miles — begins in coastal Colombo and moves steadily inland more or less east to Polgahawela Junction where the hill country begins in earnest. The Highlands section — the final four segments of track, totaling thirty miles — comprises the bulk of the journey timewise and reveals in short succession those myriad elements that render interior Sri Lanka so dynamic and exquisite. Paired against the Lowlands, the Highlands feels a world apart.

In addition to the completion of the Main Line, a seventeen-mile addendum north was added in 1880 to the cavernous town of Matale, a journey that today still takes more than one hour.

PART I: THE LOWLANDS

1. Colombo Fort to Ragama

The train snakes out of Colombo Fort yard at a patient rhythm dictated by a maze of track switches leading through all of urbanity's downsides. The polluted backside to Colombo — cramped impoverished slums absent from guidebooks and tourist brochures — happens to be one of the more colorful segments of track in the country. It is in this 12-mile stretch between Colombo Fort and Ragama Junction that we witness through an unfiltered lens the impecunious living conditions and casual habits of the vast majority of the island's population, beginning with the slums of Dematagoda where Brutalist housing projects rise from barren lots along a filthy canal and scrap-wood and sheet-metal shacks line the ever-imposing right-of-way like a tent city on some urban American sidewalk. The tracks are a triple mainline to account for almost eighty-percent of the island's daily train traffic, and, I fear, must function as a kind of constant alarm system to those who live along it due to the frequency of high-speed trains. Nevertheless, this, the busiest section of track on the island, serves also as the main footpath upon which these insolvent villagers move, wash their clothes (in the grassy area between tracks), dry their clothes (by pinning them on the rocks beside the tracks), crack coconuts (using large rocks from the track bed), and where their children congregate to fly kites and even engage in impromptu cricket matches. Track repair men can frequently be spotted wearing khaki slacks and button-down shirts, tightening and realigning the rails using handheld tools, while mothers, daughters, and grandmothers draped in colorful saris sit upon the hot iron passing the day as the train ripples past mere feet from their faces.

After crossing the mangrove-banked Kelani River rice paddies and small bucolic homesteads claim the land. Village after small village we pass through — Wanawasala, Awariyawatta, Hunupitiya, Welegoda, Enderamulla, Wattala — each with its own Buddhist temple and stately Buddha statue or enshrined bodhi tree. The land is flat and the path of the train largely straight so speed is rather rapid and we arrive in Ragama in a whirlwind of efficiency.

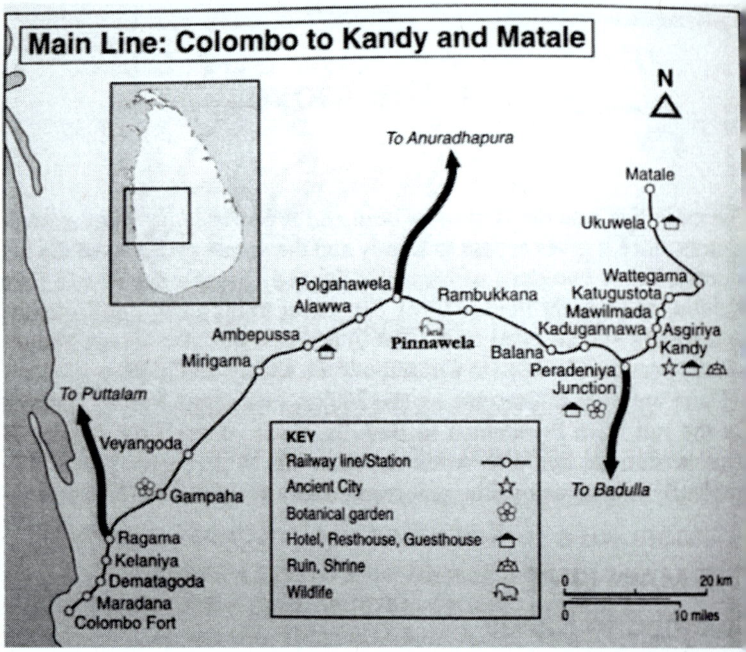

2. Ragama to Gampaha

Ragama, a minor urbanity 26 feet above sea level, is the first of three junctions on the Main Line. Here, several trains a day break north to Puttalam; all others make east past vibrant green paddies rippling in the humid breeze, coconut plantations swaying in sharp sunlight, and jungle homesteads dwelling in the shade of immense banyans. Cattle and water buffalo can frequently be spotted grazing the surrounding paddies and roaming untethered the tame land.

3. Gampaha to Veyangoda

From Gampaha (17 miles from Colombo Fort; 46-feet above sea level) we speed north-northeast, first along the Attanagalu Oya and then the Dee-al Oya, weaving through splayed-out paddies, crossing small tributary after small tributary, making good time in order to compensate for the slow climb ahead.

4. Veyangoda to Mirigama

At Veyangoda (23 miles from Colombo Fort; 61-feet above sea level) we abandon the Dee-al and begin to notice significant hills. Enfoliged knobs roll in gently around the train as we enter the Dekanda Valley, the tracks adhering to the route of the old Kandy Road nestled below precipitous cliffs that centuries prior served advantageously as ookouts for sentinels. Paddies continue to color the land, along with coconut estates, rubber estates, and small farm plots, all changing subtly with our ever-increasing elevation.

5. Mirigama to Ambepussa

At Mirigama (31 miles from Colombo; 160-feet above sea level) our speed slows considerably as track grades demand more. After crossing the Kuda Oya a massive cliff suddenly impedes us; into it the train must plunge. The first tunnel has arrived: a 400-foot-long hole bore through solid rock the top of which the eye cannot see.

6. Ambepussa to Polgahawela

Serious cliffs now begin to challenge the train's authority. We pass a wrecked, buckled, almost-split-in-half passenger car resting in rust on a steep embankment to our right and then cross the Maha Oya on a double-track steel trestle. Once across, we peer down on the increasingly rocky river from a high bank. Occasional plots of land appear black and charred and fallow, a characteristic of the hill peoples' ancient practice of slash-and-burn *chena* cultivation. Those who reside nearest the right-of-way continue to live in close relation to it, corralling the wind and otherwise utilizing the tracks with clever devise. Upon reaching Polgahawela (45 miles from Colombo) we are exactly one and a half hours into our journey and now at an elevation 244 feet above sea level.

PART II: THE HIGHLANDS

7. Polgahawela to Rambukkana

Polgahawela — meaning "coconut field" — resides at the foothills of the hill country where the jungle holds a look of dark swelter. It is the second of three junctions on the Main Line and redirects a number of

trains north into the realm of the ancient cities, as well as all trains bound for the island's eastern seaboard.

Upon departure the jungle condenses and crowds in with mutant-like largeness, the hills rising into dark cliffs poking out from the verdure like big black teeth. Steeper track grades soon become evident mainly from the inescapable exhaust fumes being emitted by the single engine as it treads into thinner atmosphere. Scattered views of the rock-strewn Maha Oya rushing below reveal rural villagers partaking in a peculiar art of washing clothes, that which Mark Twain (who traveled across the island in 1896) famously described as "a man trying to split a rock with a shirt." We pass between consecutive narrow slabs of granite at a cautionary 15 kmph. Mountains loom ahead, none more imposing than the prominent acclivity Alagalla.

8. Rambukkana to Kadugannawa

At Rambukkana the determined climb begins, slow and steady, into the once impenetrable hill country. Over the next thirteen miles the train will ascend a staggering 1,400 feet — one foot of elevation for every forty-four feet traveled. Tunnels #2 and #3 are achieved consecutively, resulting in spectacular views to the south — the most stunning yet. Upon emerging from Tunnel #4 we find the train threading across the midsection of a sheer cliff with a gaping crevice to our immediate right opposite an enormous overhanging rock face. The earth sprawls dense and verdant below with odd shaped protrusions sticking up from the canopy like islands. Tunnel #5, the longest yet at 933 feet, bathes the train in exhaust, followed by tunnels #6 and #7. Ahead, the great precipice of Alagalla reveals her eastern face in all its prominence: a vertical rise of dark granite that towers like a monument. The ancient kings, it is said, used to plunge their enemies to precipitous deaths from atop it. As the train breaches the mountain's upper strata we peer back across the valley's distinguishable landmarks: Bathalegala (also known as Bible Rock), with its a distinctive flat top like a plateau, and Utuwankanda (also known as Castle Rock), legendary hideout of Sardiel, a nefarious 19th Century bandit who was notorious for holding up carriages traveling the Kandy Road (and who time and lore have morphed into a sort of Sri Lankan Robin Hood). Alongside the tracks repurposed railroad ties serve as makeshift foot-

bridges across drainage gaps where wild and colorful flora blossom like a dedicated botanist intentioned them there. Tunnel #8 is achieved almost unnoticeably among the vivid scenery, followed by Tunnel #9 — the Moragalla Tunnel — the second longest on the island at over 1,000 feet in length. The Moragalla Tunnel leads to the Kadugannawa Incline, a treacherous section of track carved across a spectacular rock face known as Sensation Rock. A quick succession of full bore tunnels and half-tunnels ensue, each looking like a set of jaws biting down on the passing train. The most well-known of these — the Lion's Mouth — passes close enough to touch. Another inch or two of height and there would be sparks. Massive escarpments continue, forecasting the arrival of Tunnel #12, the last we shall pass through on our journey to Kandy. As we pull into Kadugannawa station (66 miles from Colombo) we have reached an elevation 1,690 feet above sea level.

9. Kadugannawa to Perendeniya

Kadugannawa station rests along a bend of track just pronounced enough that if a train possesses significant length (as often it does) the engineer at the head and brakeman at the rear cannot see one another in order to communicate via their archaic means of hand-signals when it is clear for the train to depart. In this case a station agent becomes the eyes connecting the train's front and rear. Standing mid platform in stark white uniform, the agent blows an old-fashioned bird-call whistle to commence our journey.

Homesteads ensue, each with a surrounding garden plot sprouting minimal sustenance, and often seen being attended to. We begin to follow the Nanu Oya (a rather littered section of that stream unfortunately), weaving back and forth beside arched brick viaducts put in place centuries ago by the British, and looking it. We then cross the Nanu Oya's gentle, muddy flow, only to recross it again. An overabundance of colorful blossoms along the track-bed indicate we have reached Peradeniya, the third and final junction on the line, 71 miles distant Colombo.

10. Peradeniya to Kandy

At Perendeniya Junction trains either continue northeast three miles more to Kandy or turn south into the upcountry. For us, we have not far to go, but the Mahaweli Ganga must first be crossed. The Great Sandy River, the island's longest river, remained unbridged until 1815 when the British constructed a permanent span, and not until then did the natives accept the futility of their continued resistance and ultimately cede rule to the imperialists. Once were across the river we find ourselves rolling alongside a freshly paved roadway lined with all variety of modern buildings, bus stops, super markets, and an enormous fifty-foot tall ivory-white Buddha statue backdropped by a technicolor Buddhist flag. In Kandy we alight — three and a half hours later, 74 miles distant Colombo, and 1,600 feet higher in elevation.

September 5th

Dear Sam,

In receiving this letter you are now officially in direct physical contact with the Democratic Socialist Republic of Sri Lanka (I tore the pages for this letter from a 240-page Atlas "exbook" [cheap notebook] I purchased here and it is 100% made in Sri Lanka [though I can't say for certain that *all* the materials that went into its production originated here, but probably at least like 85%, which in the U.S. makes a product "organic" (right?)]). So, from this far distant land: Hello.

I am at present in the hill country, in the town of Kandy, spending a few days just being here and not on the move. It is on a cool, gray afternoon (yes, "cool" due to Kandy's mild elevation in the island's impressive strata) that I gaze across Kandy Lake at the forested hills and am afforded the peace of mind to write you.

Kandy possesses undeniable charm. The town is very ornamental and grand, and just has a sense of pageantry pervading from it. Partly this is due to it possessing a resilient six-hundred-plus-year recorded history, and partly this is due to Kandy being not only a Buddhist mecca but also a mecca for Hindus because the two religions — take my word for it for now — are intertwined way more than I ever understood could be possible by different religions. (Ok I'll expound. See, Hindus' have a god, Upulvan, who [Hinduism is polytheistic as you probably know and different gods serve different purposes, just like Christian saints who are deemed patrons of whatever], who among other things is said to be the protector of Buddhism in Sri Lanka. See, when Buddhism first arrived here in the 3rd Century BCE, Hinduism [or some olden form of it] was the dominant religion. But with the King's conversion [it was King Tissa at the time] so went the majority of the island toward the new faith that followed the teachings of Guatama Buddha, who was an actual real documented human born in Nepal in the 6th Century BCE and who purportedly attained Nirvana [enlightenment] and thus transcended to become a Buddha, one of only four known to history [there were 3 other Buddha's, apparently — three other incarnations — but Guatama Buddha was the last and so therefore is usually referred to as the Buddha, generally speaking]. [P.S. I'm not iterating pedantic information simply because I think you don't know or understand but because I assume you are like me and that this stuff was just never as relevant or even *pal*pable, as far as grasping eastern religions goes]. So anyway, Buddhism eventually became the island's predominant religion [Theravada Buddhism — the older, more traditional form], but Hinduism *did* continue to be practiced in some areas of the island as well as remain dominant in India, and so Upulvan, honorifically I suppose, or perhaps reconciliatoraly, was deemed the protector of Buddhism on *Lanka* [an island Buddha is believed to have visited on multiple occasions]. But the more salient point I suppose is that both Buddhism and Hinduism [unlike Christianity] not only tolerate opposing religious beliefs but incorporate them into their own, Christianity included.)

... Anyway, of all the places I have been on this resplendent island, from the paradisic bays carved into the southern coast, to the dense rugged jungles and undulating tea estates of the upcountry, to the sparse, arid northwest coast, it is here in Kandy, 75 miles inland from Colombo, nestled in the mountainous foothills at a moderate 1,500-foot elevation with a perpetual chance for rain, that I think you would most appreciate. In fact, I see you here all the time, in the effortlessly beautiful Sri Lankan girls in calf-length skirts, their hair long and jet-black and often braided in twin pigtails. They are unpretentious, well-mannered and modest, and often appear in generational form walking side by side their mothers and or younger yet identical-looking sister, which is perhaps what most jolts you to the forefront of my thoughts (that and the braided pigtails).

Kandy is old by American standards. Its name is a derivative of the Portuguese word for hill — kand — and traces back to the 14th Century when the previous indigenous capital had to relocate to these hills for an amalgam of strategic and malarial-related reasons. Yet Kandy is by no means ancient by Sri Lankan standards. Listen, I am in a land boasting a documented history dating back over two thousand years. There are ruins of cities here that existed well before Anno Domini. ! Yet still, not-*so*-ancient Kandy does possess a backstory bloody enough to dwarf even the oldest American township. It happens to be a story best be told through the town's two most prominent features: the first, a manmade lake defining the southeast boundary of the city; the second, the venerated Temple of the Tooth, which abuts the lake's northern shore and is the reason for Kandy being a religious mecca. Despite their relative proximity (one practically borders the other), both embody vastly diverging significances: one is responsible for Kandy's very genesis; the other its downfall.

First, it's important to note that Sri Lanka contains zero natural lakes. However, on this island you will find an array of antiquated (and from that perspective quite impressive) massive earthen reservoirs that still to this day hold and distribute water year-round to otherwise seasonably arid regions. Kandy Lake, however, is not that type of lake. It was a rice paddy originally, and did not become a year-round body of water until around 1800 when King Vikrama Rajasinha (notice the *sinha* in his name, which means "lion" [the people are the Sinhalese]) ordered its construction after merely preferring the paddy in its flooded state. It became a permanent lake on his whim you could say. But it is this *whim* that highlights the downfall of Kandy, and with it the entire storied canon of Sinhalese kingship.

King Rajasinha, see, was a squandering, insensible ruler who the people largely distrusted and disapproved of. The inner friction his tenure caused led the chiefs of Kandy, who for centuries repelled repeated Dutch, Portuguese, and early British advances, to ultimately collude with the British in 1815 and depose of their very own king; and as Rajasinha was overthrown so went the entire Sinhalese Kingdom forever into the annals of history. (Sri Lanka, at that time called Ceylon, remained under British rule until around 1950).

Kandy Lake today, regardless of being a literal symbol of sloth and servitude (a small manmade island in the center of the lake is said to have been where King Rajasinha kept his concubine[s]), and despite being *that* proverbial stain on the city, persists as a beautiful addition to this sometimes dreary townscape, providing a constant sense of place and adding perspective to the city, as well as making for a pleasant stroll-around – the views of the surrounding hills mirroring off its surface on a clear day are most picturesque, and it serves as home to innumerous ducks and waddlers with big scabby turkey-like heads (they're actually really cute), and just *teems* with life. In there today I saw a big leatherback-looking turtle that all these children were pointing excitedly to like the marvel it was. And, all along the bank are these *enormous*-in-girth trees that must be like *really* old, and hanging around in them: wild monkeys. But I'll get to them later.

The second feature, the Dalada Maligawa, dates to the very nascence of Kandy and is a bonafide UNESCO World Heritage Site (a big deal on a global recognition and funding sort of scale). The Temple of the Tooth, as it translates, was constructed in the 16th Century not to shroud the bones of some martyr but to preserve, yes, a single tooth. The tooth is said to be that of Buddha, rescued from his funeral pyre in the 5th Century BCE. (Buddha died 483 BCE and according to at least one account a sudden heavy deluge snuffed the flames of his mode of cremation before his bones incinerated entirely and those present doled out his teeth and skeleton as treasured relics and transported these to their respective cities to be worshiped for all eternity. Sri Lanka, by way of an Indian Emperor, was said to have originally received Buddha's collar bone, and later, in the 4th Century (CE), one of his teeth.) So highly prized was this tooth that Buddhist priests fashioned imposter tooths to protect it and if they had to move it did so hidden in the hair of female monks. The tooth now resides here, in Kandy, behind the oriental-roofed temple's doors just behind where I am staying (although reportedly the tooth was confiscated sometime in the 17th C by the zealous Portuguese and destroyed. However, the Sinhalese claim that what was captured was but only another imposter and that the real tooth persists. Howeverever, Bella Woolf [the sister of Virginia Woolf's husband], in her 1907 book *Seeing Ceylon*, describes the tooth as looking something like a red-stained buffalo incisor), and (regardless the tooth's authenticity) Buddhists the world over pilgrimage yearly to Kandy to pay homage to and make offerings of lotus flowers and rupees to this one remaining earthly remnant of Buddha, especially come August when an absolutely *huge* festival called Perahera ("Parade of Parades") takes place over a span of like ten days. Perahera is a kind of Buddhist Mardi Gras: excessively extravagant and seriously ornate, with caparisoned elephants (jumbos dressed in decorated gowns — the hallmark of Southeast Asian celebratory culture) leading parades. I was in the upcountry a couple of weeks ago so I missed the actual Perahera, but I did experience a similar festival there so I feel like a got a taste of it. It's that sense of pageantry *that* pervades Kandy throughout the year.

Well it's now about 6:30 in the evening here and almost completely dark (that's one interesting thing about this place's equatorial delineation: days are neither significantly longer nor shorter despite the season, not like in the more northern hemisphere anyhow). I am staying just adjacent to the Temple of the Tooth at a place called the Olde Empire Hotel (there are still a lot of colonial British spellings hanging around with "e"s on the ends — like "centre" is pretty common). The Olde Empire, which is more hostel than hotel, faces Kandy Lake and is run by olde Sri Lankan men. I have a room on the backside of the building in a hallway all my own, a hallway with a back patio bordering the street behind (which is Colombo St.). The room is drab and barren like you'd expect a hostel room to be, but has a high ceiling so it seems more spacious, and has its own mini bathroom, which cost me a little extra (the room still only costs like $17 a night). I just ate dinner on the back patio, dinner I got from a little vegetarian hotel-in-the-wall on Colombo St. (the café/bakeries here are called "hotels"). I try to exercise my foreign purchasing power by patronizing small eateries where tourists *don't* go (I'll get to them later, along with the monkeys), but it can be frustrating, especially since I'm not familiar with the local gastronomic lingo (I'm no gourmand, as you know). Take tonight: I know I'm at a vegetarian place so I'm less leery about trying new things (although that says nothing about how relative the term vegetarian here is), but I still don't know what most items are or how to pronounce them, much less how even to order, but the word "masala" I've seen before, and seeing as how there are several variations of masala I figure it is some sort of staple worth ordering so I order the most basic sounding — "paper masala" — 'cause I remember from an Indian restaurant in Colombo that paper masala (or paper-*something*) turned out to be a thinly fried wrap of some sort, which in my Americanized mind conjured a type of crepe, or pita wrap. Additionally, I order pol roti, a pastry I see labeled in the case that looks edible (roti's similar to naan except cooked on a griddle). However, the guy working the register says that the sign's wrong and it isn't pol roti it's somethingoranother. But it still looks edible so I say OK give me two anyway; and then I notice dhal somethingoranother on the menu board, and I prefer dhal (lentil curry) to anything else so I also order the dhal thing as an accompaniment to whatever *isn't* the pol roti. But the dhal thing, it turns out, is just another kind of fried pastry, like a falafel ball. In the end I didn't know *what* I ordered, or how much it should've cost, or how I was even supposed to *eat* it. But it turned out alright. The *paper masala* came with two curries (curries to-go [called "take-away"] are put in little plastic baggies tied off at the top) and the entire order — characteristically wrapped in newspaper and handed to me like a package — cost less than three U.S. dollars. That was dinner: a big thin folded-over pastry — not really bready, more like a pancake — two mysterious vegetarian curries to soak it in (both watered-down like soup, and lukewarm), and two potatoey fried pastries. I ate it all too, and now it's dark out.

Post-sundown happens to be the time of day I most prefer here because A), I don't stand out as much and B), tourists are no longer out and about. After sundown, when the mosquitoes come out in blood-thirsty droves to feast on bare ankles, is when the island begins to shut down for the day and go into hibernation mode, which means most people cease working and start drinking. Well… most males do, at least. Anyway, if you ever find yourself in Kandy and want to know what area most resembles the fevered, gritty, market-saturated streets of the capital Colombo, it's no coincidence you need look no further than Colombo St., particularly where it runs into the western hills beneath where a great ivory-white statue of Buddha looks all-seeingly down upon the rooftops. This is where all the wine shops AKA liquor stores can be found, too. If you do ever make it to Sri Lanka, I recommend spending a few rupees at a shady local wine shop just after dusk. They're like gambling dens, the poor hawking their hard-earned day's earnings on "strong" beer (basically malt liquor) and *arrack* (distilled coconut toddy aged in barrels like whiskey), the locals' spirit-of-choice. Once you've thrusted yourself into the local mercantilian frenzy to negotiate a brew — patrons stepping forward with Sri Lankan Dutch courage demanding to know just what you want so they can aid in negotiating the transaction to some benefit of their own damaged dharma — your cultural immersion becomes that much more complete and your own spirit enhanced by contributing directly to the livelihood of the natives. This, in turn, may help you to realize their way of life really not all that different from yours; that you're just as capable of interfacing with them as they with you. Thus, you grow less timid and as a result your experiences become much richer. I tell you this because you likely won't find this advice (nor the lower part of Colombo St.) in any guidebook, which brings me back to the tourists.

Certainly a huge downside to Kandy and its festive aura is that it is year-round infested with tourists forever optimistic young backpackers. This is mainly evident due to the fact that the local population here does not drown out foreign travelers like in Colombo. Instead, the town seems one-third white (including many obvious tour groups), and always (I mean I could bet a testicle on this) there's a copy of Lonely Planet's *Guide to Sri Lanka* involved. I've silently come to loath the sight of these clichéd sightseers, each with their noses a few dust mites away from the same lame guidebook. Come to think of it, this damn Olde Hotel is probably guidebook recommended because I'm just now becoming aware of all the backpacking couples coming and going (I'm now sitting on the hotel's front balcony, a common area). The reason I find this annoying — all the tourists here in Kandy — is because I can't stand thinking I'm trapped in the same funnel of experience as everyone else, but also, I admit, I envy their companionship (it's been more than difficult traveling alone over here — far more difficult than I am able to convey on paper from such great distance, which is probably why this letter is so long). But, as an upside, these overly blatant tourists do render me, a non-backpack-toting loner (I ditched the backpack after my last trip and now just carry what I wear and what fits in my small camera bag), less a target for solicitation, and as a result I don't get bothered half as much, which is truly a welcome relief! But tourists are not the only thing Kandy is infested with. The other nuisance (and this I promised I'd address): monkeys.

Depending on if you're a Kandy resort owner, banana vendor, or Western traveler wholly unaccustomed to the wild variability of the jungle (as am I), these feral creatures can prove either pest (albeit fairly large and cunning and brazen ones that strikingly resemble *us*) or nature's marvel. I no doubt understand the commercial Kandyan's plight in dealing with them but my sympathies are lent to the primates – I find them fantastic! Enter last evening: I take a stroll along the lake to acquaint myself with its contours, and toward the back, after having passed into the "Sacred City Limit," my attention turns to what I sense is a tree branch to my left suddenly breaking off from above and falling. Not so. Tis a troop of wild monkeys, the precise genus of which evades me but doubtless descending the well-weighed-down branch onto a pile of refuse for a rapid snatch-and-grab within some fenced-in enclosure. Before I know it monkeys are scrambling toward me and scaling the rusty chain-links in front of me to hoist themselves into the branches directly above my head, one of the apes grasping the booty in its paw: a hand of bananas. Suddenly, a finger snaps free and falls on my side of the fence, tumbles down a hillside of exposed tree roots, dirt, and rock, and settles an arm's length from me on the walking path. What do I do? I pick up the prized fruit; but before I know it three monkeys have descended after it and are approaching me Velociraptor-like – from each side *and* the center. The center monkey (whom I take to be the Alpha) approaches ever so brazenly with a nonchalant determination I have known few humans to possess. As it inches ever closer to reclaim the rightful prize – me holding the banana out for it to recapture – I suddenly notice a smaller, commensal primate attached to the bosom, clinging inverted to its mother's tummy; and in my amazed stupor at that sight the matron, without hesitation, takes the banana from my hand, turns and effortlessly re-ascends the tree to safety followed by the others. Un-fucking-real, I thought.

Take care Sam, I will hopefully see you soon.

Aa

Street Scene, Kandy

Monkeys

Kandy rail yard

Kandy Lake

Temple of the Tooth

Colombo Street (looking west)

PART III: MATALE LINE

Raining. Clothes now wet. Body itching from cheap hostel. Train still at station. Slowly filling. Mostly mothers and daughters and families with young children. No tourists. Kandy is the end of the line for them. No need to go further north to Matale. Train horn sounding. Loud engine revving. Could be us. More revving. Still no movement. Another horn somewhere outside. Guy coming through selling newspapers. Train opposite us now moving south. Probably back to Colombo. Or could be going to Nawalapitiya and on to Badulla. Lots of tourists on that train probably. Damn bedbugs. Must be. Wasn't expecting that. Should not pay for the room after all. Think about it. Would be bad karma. But fucking mosquito eating me all night too. And now measle-like things all over my body that I thought was some strange fever or disease at first. Dinging sound. Means an announcement's going to be made. Can't understand what's being said. Might be an announcement for this train to depart. Still on time at two. Open my window when the train gets moving. Little girl in a pretty little prom-dress. Very colorful and fancy dress for a little girl. Somewhere in the world there's always a cell-phone ringing. Guy selling newspapers again. No I do not want a Sinhala newspaper. Guy selling popcorn or something too. I might buy some pineapple if that guy comes through. Starting to feel nauseous because of the rain. Hope that gets better once we're moving. New room when I get back I'll demand. No more bedbugs. Wonder if they're in my clothes? Popcorn Man a*gain*. Should be in Matale in an hour. That Buddha statue on the hill. Would be nice to be up there in the clouds right now. Wonder can I climb up there? Another day. What's this guy selling? Oh. Lottery tickets. No thanks. He's wearing a nametag thing. Guess he's licensed. I'm the only non-Sri Lankan on this train probably. I'll see in Matale. Probably raining there too. Would be nice if not though. Ancient cave-temple something like two miles north of town. Fucking goddamn bedbugs. Should have known. Distant horn sounding. Didn't bother buying a ticket for this train. No need. I'll just give them an old expired ticket in Matale if I need to. They never look. Everybody must do it. No no trespassing on railroad tracks in Sri Lanka. Veritable paths on which to walk and explore. Popcorn Man again. White-bearded old men. Children. Orange-robed monks. All use the tracks like a sidewalk. Through tunnels even. Tunnel just past the station in Kandy I walked through yesterday. Guy peeing in there as I came out. Never really see Sri Lankans peeing in public like you see people doing everywhere in The States. More modest. Cow-shit all over the roads though. Soldiers in Kandy today. Day before there was not. Then last night suddenly a military presence on street corners and around the Temple. Guy started following me around the lake after dark trying to talk to me. Where am I staying? Second night in a row. Learned my lesson in Weligama. People preying on me. Feel sorry for the tourists who fall for that cloying. No thanks here. Mustn't be two o'clock yet. Kid across the aisle laughing. So joyous. Horn sounding somewhere ahead. People still moving through the car. Popcorn Man still speaking rapidfire Sinhala trying to sell popcorn. Bedbugs still bugging me.

Wonder if I can get rid of them just by showering or if they'll be in my clothes till I can do laundry. If so will I'll *ever* get them out? Feel bad about B's laundry. That grease crayon in with my stuff marking up all her clothes. Did that to Sam's laundry too. My clothes don't matter. Already holey and stained and filthy and colorless. Popcorn Man again. Doesn't look like he's sold any. *Habbapognisci* it sounds like he's saying. Guess I'll leave Kandy tomorrow. Train back to Colombo and do some laundry and get ready to go north to the ancient-ruin cities. Almost half done with all the rail lines in the country. Just have Anuradhapura and Trinco and Batti to go. Long rides. Then might go back up to Uva and stomach the tourists in Nuwara Eliya or Ella. Maybe Hatton too to see or possibly climb Adam's Peak. Train car now full. Wonder when the last train back to Kandy is? Take a bus from Matale maybe. Buses not so bad. Just nauseating in the rain. And always cramped and crowded. New room too when I get back. Different bed. No bugs. Here comes a blue commuter train like the one I arrived from Colombo on two days ago. Probably what this train is waiting for to depart. We departed Colombo at 10:35 and it's a three-and-a-half-hour ride so that makes perfect timing. Yes some are transferring. Should be departing soon. School boys in white suits board. More families. No one wants to sit next to me it seems. I wouldn't object. Doesn't bother me unless it's some tout trying to use me. Train car now really crowded. Seat next to me taken by a suitcase. Now a body. Damn popcorn vendor *again*. Looks like he's holding some twenties though so maybe sold some. Should be departing momentarily. Cell-phone ringing. Or possibly being turned on. Heavy sky'll make for pretty photos at least. Except . . . train horn sounding – now moving . . . except that I'm on the west side of the car where the sky is bright and may appear blown-out in photos. Buddha's up there on the hill too. Moving slowly. Ramba music playing. Think of all the leeches out there in the tall grass and jungle scrub. Glad I haven't yet acquired another. Bedbugs worse though. Can't see them. Can't get rid of them. Stopping just outside the yard. Probably so the brakeman in the last car can close over the tracks a gate which restricts entrance to the yard. Guy-next-to-me's phone ringing. Indian music throbbing. Moving again. Creeping slowly beneath the first bridge. Probably difficult to gain traction on the wet rails. Give it some sand. Political posters beneath the bridge torn and faded. No graffiti though. Could go without the diesel exhaust today. Hope not too many tunnels on the way. Train barely moving. Pulling hard. Having trouble I think. Engine heaving. Station under cover but out here it's wet and the wheels probably unable to gain traction. Definitely an incline. Not even one mile per hour. Ten km/h the speed limit. No p. Wonder what they're going to do. Back up and start over? Engineer probably just trying to make it to the first tunnel where it's dry and the wheels can catch. Sorta like being stuck in mud with only two-wheel-drive. Or snow. Seven-hundred-dollar towing bill for Richie. Modern railroads don't have this problem but Sri Lanka is a land stuck in time. Railroad especially antiquated. Still using tokens and lanterns. Sesquicentennial just about. Passengers sticking their heads out the windows wondering *What the Hey*.

Little cascade running down a granite trackside wall. Can't see the first tunnel yet but now at the second overpass. Well-faded posters beneath. Muslim guy standing up on a bridge stoic and proud looking while beside him several kids stand beneath a common umbrella peering down on the train. Slowly moving. Ramba music still playing. Wild green vines sprouting verdantly out of every hole in the trackside wall. Out then up. Smells like waffle-cones all of a sudden. Briefly. Huge bo-tree on the hill. Sacred probably. Five-hundred-years old at least. The brim of my hat drips from the rain coming in through the window. Train not going fast enough to prevent that. Window must be dripping bad though because the guy behind me wants it closed he just tapped me on the shoulder to say. Should be a short ride to Matale. If the train makes it. If not I can walk back to Kandy. Not far. But moving more rapidly now it seems. Yes. Increasing speed. Another overpass. Two teens huddled beneath an umbrella under the bridge beside the tracks facing the wall. Boy and girl. Kids here always going to shady spots to cuddle and flirt it seems. The first station we stop at is more like a bus-stop. Way dilapidated. And there's shit on the ground and a shit-rag above it on the bench. Someone was very ill. School girls in saintly white dresses board. Their implied purity tainted by the presence of that human feces. Crossing gates sounding ahead. Along with vehicle horns of course. Picking up speed into the first tunnel. Slowly. Now out the other end and into a narrow green ravine. Foliage encroaching. Closely. School kids laughing as they move through the car. Second station. Muslim girls in stark white hijabs board. Less than a minute that stop. But if every half mile this trip could be long. Trackside shacks appropriate corrugate-metal roofing. Probably to catch water. Road slick today. Good thing Kandy has functioning crossing-gates. Such pretty hill country. Such tower-

ing verdant palms. Cream-colored coconuts clustered up beneath like retracted testicles. Interesting job to get those down. Can't just wait till they fall. Coconut Man comes every couple weeks Lal says. That's the man who scales the trunk machete in mouth and hacks down the coconuts. Collects the toddy as payment probably. Then sells it to distillers. Many buildings in Kandy painted with thick vertical red and white stripes. Like a candy-cane. Even telephone-poles in Sri Lanka look ancient. Like ancient technology. Lines aboveground of course. Not much remodeling happening here. Too preoccupied with staying alive amid often-violent political upheaval. Temples and more temples. *Maligawas* they're called in Sinhala. Most rain I've seen in this country today. Not even monsoon season either. Just a rainy part of the country. Wonder how many trains a day to Matale and back? Could take a tuk-tuk. Or two or three. Wouldn't be worth it though. Crossing the Mahaweli Ganga again (the first of three prophecies fulfilled). Gorgeous lush hill country. Katugastota. Still trying to break the names of these towns into root-words. "Tota" I've heard before. Bentota. Must be some variation of village. Or a reference to the main geographic feature. Maybe it means "located on a river." Both "totas" on a major river. Now crossing another river. Couldn't be the Mahaweli. Not wide enough. Haven't heard from Popcorn Guy in a while. Maybe he got off already or maybe he stayed in Kandy. The window ledge those little girls are putting their mouths and faces on must be filthy. Probably have better immune systems over here. Americans take all kinds of vaccines. Especially before traveling outside the country. No vaccines for me. Glad current malady's probably just bedbugs. Have been getting some weird sicknesses though. Strange sicknesses. That weird broken-foot pain I had where I couldn't walk for a day but that dissipated the next only to crawl up my calf as a nasty muscle cramp but that is now no more. That sleepless night I spent near-paralyzed from intestinal cramps clearly incurred from blasted Naan Man naan. Threw everything up in violent paroxysms and the next day was fine. Stomach does frequently feel diarrheic and cramped though. Probably not eating at all the cleanliest places. Too high-end for me. Prefer small hotel' roti and dhal. Too stubborn and abashed though to renege on an order if it's cold. Like this morning. Probably leftovers from the night before. Not too smart to eat. Flies always buzzing. Depositing larva wherever they land. Maggots. Can't find a cup of coffee usually that's decent either. Nice laxative in the morning. French Press place too expensive. Four-hundred twenty rupees. More than a cup of Wandering Goat coffee. Wouldn't mind Rupa bothering me though. Wonder how much those girls earn anyway? Thought about asking her. Ridiculous for me to order a cup of coffee that costs more than they make an hour. Wonder what minimum wage here is? Rude to ask. Doesn't seem to be taxes on items either. Just bottle deposits on glass bottles and aluminum cans. Beer cheaper than coffee. Weird not tipping either. Westerners probably still tip in Kandy. Probably Rupa thinks I'm cheap not tipping. Still haven't figured it out entirely. Banana trees. Fig trees. Tea bushes. Palm trees. Outstanding oriental flora probably brought over by the British. Still botanical

gardens around. Probably not as kept up anymore. Great clouds hang over the mountains ahead. Mountains over 5,000 feet. That's 2,000 plus meters I think (hard to tell). Can't remember the conversion ratio from meters to feet. Should know it. Can't remember Celsius to Fahrenheit either. 27 degrees Celsius yesterday. Huge wading water-buffalo with multiple birds perched on its back. So many derelict little buildings and railroad shacks along the right-of-way. Wattegama. "Gama" means "jungle" I think. *The Village In The Jungle* set in Beddegama. Probably isn't written biographically. Although so much truth. Depressing book. All the characters die of disease or broken-hearts. Their pets taken as bad omens and stoned in front of their eyes. The girls raped. What horrible hardship. *Veddas*. Still here too. Yatewata. "Wata" must mean something jungle related. Jungle very dense and steep. It's a wonder this land was ever probed and settled. Homesteads all over the place though. In every nook and crevice and on the steepest of acclivities. Overgrown though. Forests no longer virgin primeval. Hacked up too much. *Chena*ized. Slashed and burned. Scrub reclaimed. That's why monkeys are so angry. People harvest all the fruit and transport it to towns. Like Patampaha. Monkeys must go where the food is. Not their fault. People crowd into cities where jobs are. Small towns die. Then flee to the suburbs when towns get too crowded and crime-riddled. Gentrifies everything. Then move back to town and displace the poor to the suburbs where everything's more expensive. Model of American inefficiency. Still small villages in Sri Lanka. Villages in the jungle. Primitive husbandry. Small footprints on the land. Amazing that the majority of the population here still lives rural. Train really rollicking now. Must be on a decline. Heavy fog and clouds bisecting the mountains east. Knuckles Mountains. Little kid trying to put his window back up now that the rain has ceased. Nothing to see out my side except steep jungle so vibrant green it's headaching. Guy across from me keeps repeating very corny-like but friendly "What's your country?" even though I'm not looking at him. Kids outside the train yell at it as it passes. Feral hill country. Nothing pruned. Stations more frequent. Train car now almost completely empty. What's-your-country Guy still trying to initiate generic conversation. Rain picks back up. Train stops. High-pitched whistle blows. Engineer sticks his head out the front looking to the caboose for the OK to move on. Talk about primitive. Wonder if they even have cell-phones to call each other if necessary. Or does one of them have to wave the green or red flag if problems arise and then walk to the opposite end of the train? Damn fly bothering me. First bedbugs now flies. Trees with above-ground-forming roots that look like bony emaciated hands. Ukawela. Now seeing tuk-tuks again. Must mean were close. Population correlates directly to number of tuk-tuks present at any given time. Can't be tuk-tuks in some of these villages where roads are not and only paths are worn into the muddy hillsides. Too steep. Elwela. Two-lane road bordering the tracks. Tuk-tuk. Motorbike. Primitive rail crossing. There goes a bus. Must be on its way to Kandy. Bus every half-hour from Kalpitiya to Puttalam they told me. Must at least be that frequent here. Not even as far. Still probably takes an hour. Probably sits alongside the road for half an hour someplace to kill time. Extra pay. Passengers now take their belongings down. Matale next probably. Not many people left on the train. Five people only in the car. A father. A mother. A son. Me. And What's-your-country Guy. Bananas grow so oddly. Beautiful phallic purplish mauve flowers drooping out the bottoms of bunches. More urbanity. Looks like the outskirts of Kandy. Mile 2147. Matale.

6. Northern Line

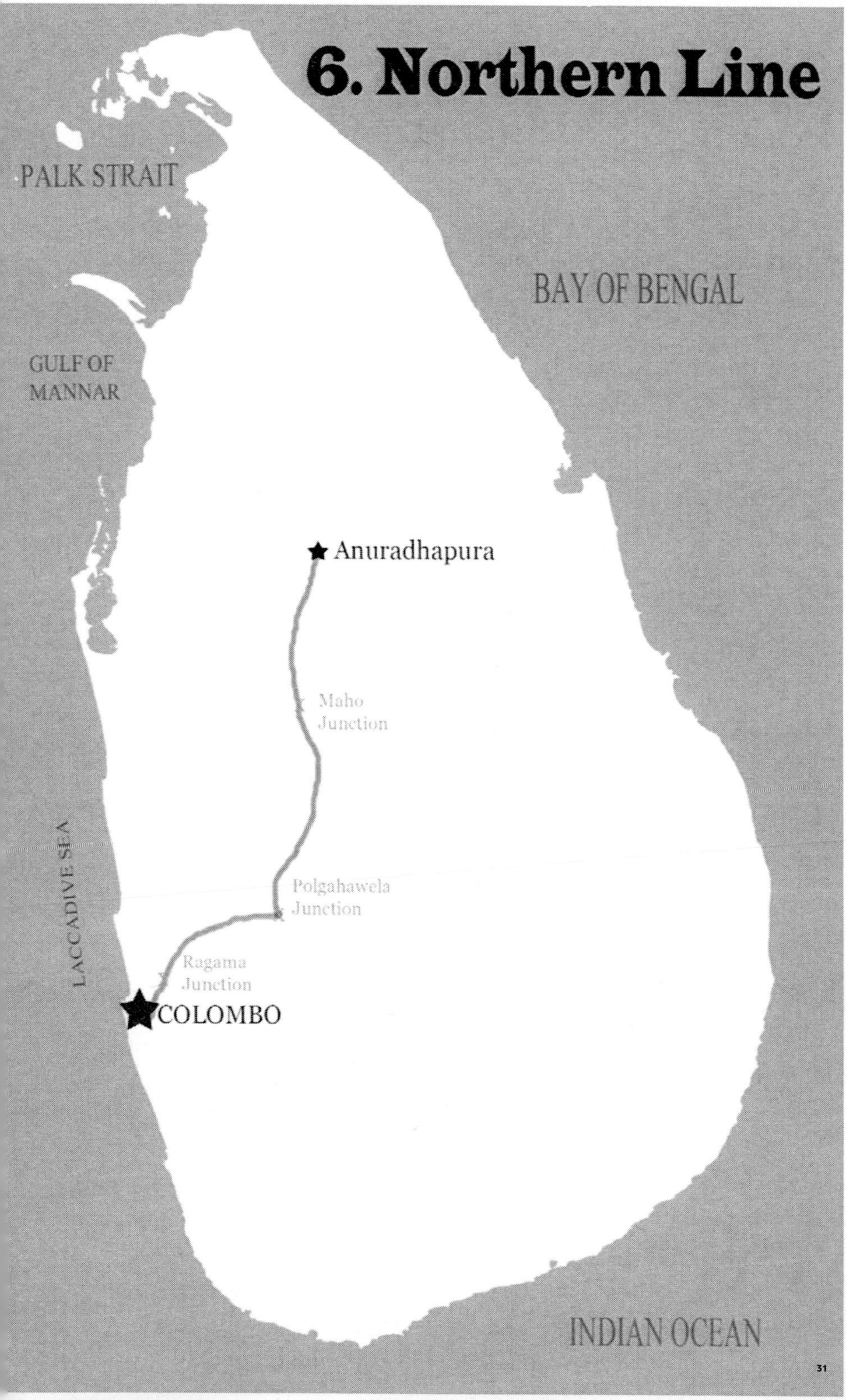

ANURADHAPURA

He, he fearless wayfarer, who in olden times traversed many great yojana, in the full-moon light of Assayuja, (he) went thither on the iron palanquin to, on the fair bank of Malawatu, the sacred city Anuradha.

TRAIN: Rajarata Rajini (Queen of the North-Central Region).
DESTINATION: Anuradhapura.
ROUTE: Main Line and Northern Line.
DISTANCE: 81 Miles (from Polgahawela Junction).
DURATION: 3 Hours 45 Minutes.
TIME OF DEPARTURE: 1518.
TOWNS AND VILLAGES SERVED: Girambe, Tallawattegedera, Potuhera, Naliiya, Kurunegala, Wallawa, Ganewatta, Hariyah, Nagollagama, Maho, Ambampola, Galgamuna, Ottukulama, Senarathgama, Tambuttegama, Talawa, Sravasthipura, New Town, Anuradhapura...
TERRAIN: Hilly and semi-mountainous, giving way to pastures, paddies and farmland.
CLIMATE AND CONDITIONS: Hot, humid, and on this particularly overcast day, severely rainy, the normally dry, red earth puddling up around the trackbed.
SCENERY: Mopeds parked on a dirt road beside a field where children play pick-up cricket; cattle grazing along the right-of-way, in rice paddies and meadows, some tethered by rope, others roaming freely; women in saris standing on the bund of an earthen reservoir rinsing themselves while cattle graze the grassy shore; a man emerging from the woods carrying a stack of bark chips balanced on his head; a man standing in a pond in front his home, the water milky white and the man — wearing only a sarong — using a bucket on a string to scoop water with which to rinse himself; men in fields threshing; dogs chasing after the train; villagers standing in their doorways watching the steel wheels roll past; random acts of primitive husbandry...
NOTEWORTHY SIGHTS: An 88-foot-tall Buddha statue atop a towering rock face overlooking the town of Kurunegala, followed by a spine of enormous black rocks rising 800-feet above the jungle, each bearing in name its ancestral zoomorphic resemblance: Elephant, Tortoise, Beetle, Eel, Goat, Crocodile, and the highest of all: Yakdessagala, or She-Demon's curse.
TIME OF ARRIVAL: 1905.

*

The settlement of Anuradhapura, which reigned as the religious and political capital of the island for fourteen-hundred years, first rose to prominence in 377 BCE when King Pandukabhaya (the 5th king to take the throne) declared it the new capital of the Sinhalese Kingdom — then known as Rajarata — relocating from the more vulnerable coastal vicinity of present-day Mannar.

In 247 BCE[1] Anuradhapura saw an important new king ascend to the throne: Devanampiyatissa, the second son of the previous king Mutasiva. Tissa, as he is colloquially known, became acquainted with the Mauryan Emperor Ashoka (268 - 232 BCE) whose empire covered a large portion of modern India, and early in his reign received on the island the emperor's son Mahinda who brought with him the teachings of Buddha in the form of a new religion. Thus, Tissa spearheaded a mass religious conversion in which 40,000 people were said to be converted in a single day. This, in time, effectively turned the capital into an urban monastery of sorts. To add to the city's decor a sapling from the very bodhi tree under which Buddha gained enlightenment was gifted to the king by the emperor. The tree was transplanted with lavish ceremony and obsessive symbolism, and around it Anuradhapura blossomed and grew into a city of great religious significance and advanced culture.

At its height Anuradhapura was home to an estimated two million people, and as its legend and mystique spread across Asia and into Europe, relics pertaining to the Buddha sought refuge in both the city's remoteness and its unilateral devotion to the new religion. Great monuments were erected to honor and house these relics, such that the world had never seen: massive balanoid structures composed entirely of brick that rival the Egyptian Pyramids in size and ancient wonder. These *stupas* (known as *dagabas* to the Sinhalese) have come to epitomize ancient Sinhalese culture the world over.

Concurrent to Anuradhapura's growth the Sinhalese flourished into a highly civilized society, one both technologically advanced and culturally exclusive. The ancient Sinhalese diverted rivers great distances, stored rainwater for the dry seasons, devised filters for potability, and developed underground piping and a rudimentary sewage system. To this day the plains outlying the city reveal a network of massive earthen reservoirs complete with

[1]. Some texts date Tissa's rule beginning as early as 307 BCE. More commonly, he is said to have come to power in 288 BCE. However, many core associations between Tissa and Buddhism's emergence on the island have been linked to the reign of Ashoka and few doubt the two kings were contemporaries. Therefore, this writer adheres to the more conservative date corresponding to the Mauryan Emperor's rule.

bunds, dikes, and interconnecting sluice channels, all of which illustrate a clear understanding of complex hydrology as well as a propensity toward intensive agriculture.

When Anuradhapura eventually succumbed to abandonment in the late 10th Century it was a result of relentless contestation from foreign invaders (mostly Chola-Tamils from modern-day India); the kingdom relocated to Polonnaruwa, a more defense-oriented site sixty miles to the southeast. For Anuradhapura the next 900 years became a period of prolonged hibernation, subjecting its stunning architecture and engineering accomplishments to the punishing pertinence of the jungle and an occasional thorough pillaging at the hands of obstinate suzerains.

Fastforward to the 19th Century: The British, after wresting control of the island's perimeter from the Dutch, upon one of their subsequent probes into the interior (an area the Dutch and Portuguese prodded willfully but never fully controlled), rediscovered the remarkable ruins of one of the greatest ancient cities in the world, one that the rest of the world knew precious little of. Before them lay the 2,000-year-old architectural skeleton of a 16-mile-wide city with a deep and well-documented history etched into its elaborate friezes and the very bricks of the structures that defined it.

By the early 1900s large-scale renovations were underway and Anuradhapura's significance began to seep back into public consciousness enough to affect national identity. Yet it would be another eighty years before Anuradhapura won global recognition and was awarded UNESCO World Heritage Site status, and by then the island, finally rid of its European colonizers, had become engulfed in its own internecine conflict.

With a defiant Tamil insurgency claiming the region north of Anuradhapura as their rightful homeland, Eelam, and the Sri Lankan Army pushing back fiercely from the south, the sacred city once again found itself wedged in the middle of a violent, ethnically charged conflict. Thankfully, much of the ruins were spared major destruction, but not until after the war ultimately ended in 2009 did Anuradhapura emerge from the gloomy shadows of extremism and radiate its true brilliance once more.

Maha Bodhi- 3rd Century BCE

The oldest historically documented tree in the world is not as enormous as I expected, that is until realizing that the spectacle surrounding it, while respectfully reverent, dwarfs the tree itself. A fifteen-foot-high stone wall surrounds the base of the tree entirely (originally intended to protect it from foraging elephants) while a perimeter army of its saplings — all quite old now themselves — shield the crown from damaging winds. Four ornate stone staircases — eighteen steps each framed by duel "guard-stones" and with intricate semi-circular "moonstones" as the base — ascend the wall from each side (the four cardinal directions). From atop the wall a balcony of altars look down on the tree's roots. The tree has three main branches, each crutched on a golden pedestal; its various limbs are draped with Buddhist prayer flags like at a Himalayan base-camp. Its trunk remains an alter unto itself: pilgrims drop rupees onto its roots like at a wishing well, bestow flowers upon it like at a grave, face it with hands pointed to the sky and fingertips pressed to their foreheads in entranced prayer. They caress the trunks of its offspring, picnic and pray in its imperial shade. Not a leaf falls that is not collected as memento.

It is well documented that this tree, known as the Maha Bodhi (Great Bodhi Tree), is a direct descendent of the very same bodhi tree that stood in Bodh Gaya, India in the 6th Century BCE beneath which one Siddhartha Gautama obtained enlightenment and graduated to Buddhahood, effectively becoming *the* Buddha. As a sapling (said to be the south branch), the tree was sent down the river Ganges circa 240 BCE[2] under the care of a Buddhist nun. It was then transported to the island by boat and received em-

[2]. Ironically, much confusion and conflicting dates surround the documentation of the oldest historically documented tree in the world. In fact, one of the more difficult tasks associated with writing this book has been settling on a reliable time-line in order to pinpoint the exact year of this heralded tree's planting. While the majority of texts (including most local ones) mark the year of its planting to be 288 BCE, it is also a core association that King Tissa receieved and planted the tree on behalf of the Indian Emperor Ashoka who's rule did not begin until 268 BCE — twenty years *after*. John Davy, a British doctor who lived on the island for three years shortly after the British became its sole rulers, in his book, *An Account of the Interior of Ceylon*, dates the branch's arrival at 236 AB (After Buddha), which corresponds to 247 BCE (Buddha died in 483 BCE). This seems a more reliable date.

phatically by the newly converted King Tissa who carefully selected an auspicious date to plant the tree and then did so emblematically in the center of the city. For more than 2,250 years this tree has stood and thrived in miraculous constant bloom. It has witnessed countless wars, repeat invasions, and persisted through a millennium of relative abandonment. Upon its subsequent rediscovery by the British come the early 19th Century it was the only living connection to the ancient city.

Ruanweli Dagaba- 2nd Century BCE

Three monumental stupas rise from the jungles of Anuradhapura, each visible from a distance. King Dutugamunu (161 – 137 BCE) is credited with overseeing construction of the first great stupa: the Ruanweli (Gold Dust) Dagaba — 338-feet tall with a 950-foot circumference. The ancient Egyptians would have gawked at such an impressive edifice outside the deserts of Cairo, one that unlike their pyramids seemed to defy the laws of gravity with its convex contours. Yet the function of the Ruanweli differed wildly from the intricate function of their own monuments, for no deceased monarch lay entombed within, but rather a small invaluable treasure pertaining to a holy man not even of the island.

The Ruanweli is said to have originally contained a sapling grafted from the Maha Bodhi bedecked with emeralds, coral, silver and gold, along with various precious offerings, all encased within an eight-inch-thick stone receptacle encapsulated by a second enclosure then sealed off from the world behind a layer of bricks forming a dome more-than four-hundred-feet thick. A square minaret (known as a *hti*) was constructed atop the dome and capped with a cylindrical neck sporting a long, slender spire. A ten-inch-thick waterproof sealant of lime plaster was then applied to complete the stupa. When rediscovered by the British in the early 1800s the Ruanweli lay half-buried in alluvial soil, its white plaster exterior fully worn away and, in its place, a veritable miniature forest sprouting healthily from the bricks. Awed by the artistry revealed in what they had begun to excavate, the British soon came to view the Ruanweli as a national monument rather than a mere religious structure. Large-scale restoration was to follow.

A wide, newly-paved walkway leads from the Maha Bodhi to the Ruanweli, which regardless the direction one approaches appears uniform — only the background changes, along with the light, which makes the Ruanweli something of an enormous convex sundial (or a celestial monument perhaps). Following the path, I first come to a number of stone columns (once the interior of a portico) just in front a perimeter of flagpoles hoisting the official Buddhist flag (a flag conceptualized by Sri Lankan Buddhists in 1885). Beyond stands an elaborate retaining wall, ten-feet in height, depicting a row of elephants, each life-sized and sculpted identically, seeming to both guard the Ruanweli as well as hold the structure atop their backs. This awesome feature — made up of more than four-hundred elephants total, said to have originally contained rubies for eyes and actual ivory tusks — wraps completely around the squarish platform from which rises the axisymmetric brick dome of the Ruanweli: cloud-white and bell-shaped with a copper spire pointing to the cerulean sky. Three levels of concentric stone friezes terracing inward around the base of the dome help stabilize it, each intricately detailed with lions, servants, elephants, lotus flowers, geese, playful baby elephants whose trunks flail up down left and right. The tiniest, subtlest aspects seem to bear enormous significance.

Jetavana Dagaba- 3rd Century CE

Outside the realm of the Ruanweli lie a sea of ruins strewn about like an untended to cemetery. Staircases prefaced by museum-worthy guardstones today lead to lonely trees sprouting from patches of regularly mowed grass where visiting locals picnic among jaded lemurs, eating with their hands from unfolded newspaper wrappings of rice and curry. From here I follow a red dirt path across a small clear creek, through a city block of old geometric brick-and-stone building foundations, and toward the towering half-broken brick spire of the Jetavana Dagaba[3].

At the time of its completion in the late 3rd Century the Jetavana was by far the tallest monument in Anuradhapura, rising 450-feet above the earth. Its unique "paddy-heap" shape differs subtly in form from the bubble shaped Ruanweli, and this slightly augmented design affords it superior tensile strength. When examined by the British in the 19th Century the Jetavana's dome showed little wear, remarkable considering the centuries in which it bore the additional weight of an entire suspended ecosystem.

At present the Jetavana stands only 400-feet tall, yet it remains one of the largest brick structures in the world. Its sheer volume in bricks — 40-million square feet — would be enough to build a railway tunnel twenty miles long, or a wall ten-feet in height stretching from Los Angeles to San Francisco. But without the same degree of

---

[3]. Many older maps confuse the Jetavana Dagaba with Anuradhapura's third main stupa, the near-identical looking Abhayagiriya Dagaba (albeit retaining respective histories), to the extent that in hindsight this author was seriously confused regarding which dagaba was actually located at which end of the ancient city. That is until he went back through his photographs and saw that he had smart-thinkingly photographed the official plaque denoting the Jetavana the Jetavana, and so of course he goes by that.

restorative attention awarded the Ruanweli (no white plaster coats the exterior and no throng is present to pilgrimagingly worship) the Jetavana possesses the silent air of a forgotten structure.

Dakkhina Stupa- 1st Century BCE

Just south of the oldest historically documented tree on earth, on a grassy knoll between two forking roads, I come upon the crumbling remains of a cylindrical brick hovel five five stories in height. Ancient inscriptions on the structure (although indecipherable to me) identify this as the Dakkhina Stupa (Southern Dagoba) and trace its creation to the reign of King Valagamba (89 to 77 BCE). While few argue as to the Dakkhina's purpose — it was built to immortalize a great king — much speculation surrounds *which* great king the Dakkhina was intended to honor. As recently as the 20th Century the Dakkhina was known as Elara's Tomb, built atop the spot where King Elara perished in battle. However, Elara was Tamil, and this may have contributed to a change of Sinhalese heart regarding tradition because no longer is the Dakkhina said to mark the site of Elara's defeat but instead to contain the ashes of a Sinhalese who not only succeeded Elara to the throne but who proved to be the very individual to decide his fate. It seems the two, although several millennia removed, remain bitter adversaries.

Elara, a Chola-Tamil from the Malabar (eastern) coast of India, invaded the island in 205 BCE and overthrew King Asela. He then proceeded to rule Anuradhapura for an unprecedented forty-four years. To his credit Elara was largely viewed as a just and fair ruler; his shortfall was that as a Hindu he did not treat Buddhism with the same precedence as his predecessors, and this was considered blasphemous to the Sinhalese who viewed themselves safekeepers of the religion. In 161 BCE a long-coming revolt mounted from the south led by a young Sinhalese from royal lineage

named Dutugamunu. A direct challenge was made to Elara and the two met in grandiose combat mounted on war elephants, and if conventional wisdom is to be held correct, the site of that epic confrontation, at which Elara ultimately fell to his death, is none other than where the Dakkhina now stands. Dutugamunu commenced to rule Anuradhapura for the next twenty-four years and ushered in one of the most prosperous and prolific periods in the island's history.

From a distance the Dakkhina appears diminutive, a dull mound of bricks. No parapet of earth elevates the structure and no stone walkway heralds approach. Furthermore, no guard stands on watch and nothing mandates the removal of headwear or sandals. Most surprising, however, is that nothing prohibits my climbing upon it, which I do; and although ascending the stupa requires a fully vertical ascent in places, it is nonetheless manageable due to how the Dakkhina has devolved to resemble a wraparound staircase in parts (which may be more of a clue as to how it was constructed). From atop the structure, uneven ruins protrude gently from beneath an undulating carpet of patina grass. The air is refreshingly breezy and devoid of insects, and the view afforded from slightly above the jungle canopy reveals five visible stupas, several expansive reservoirs, and contours of roads leading to all.

Mirisewetiya Dagaba- 2nd Century BCE

The Mirisewetiya, at 120-feet tall and 560-feet in circumference, was not Anuradhapura's first stupa — that honor goes to the Thuparama Dagaba, constructed a century earlier — but the Mirisewetiya was the island's first bubble-shaped stupa, a design that merits attention for being found nowhere else in the Buddhist world. Local legend relates that the exact location of the Mirisewetiya came to be as a result of a mysterious occurrence happened upon the king. King Dutugamunu, who was known to carry a scepter containing a relic from Buddha, one day inserted his scepter into the ground whilst he detoured down to the reservoir to bathe, and upon returning discovered that the scepter could not be removed from the ground for whatever mystical reason. Always the spiritualist, Dutugamunu took this as a Sign and ordered a structure built overtop the scepter in order to preserve the relic. This became the Mirisewetiya. Furthermore, legend relates that Dutugamunu conjured the particular architectural conception of the Mirisewetiya after observing a soapy bubble sitting on the surface of the water. Like a visual artist, the king sought to reconstruct the image on a much grander scale.

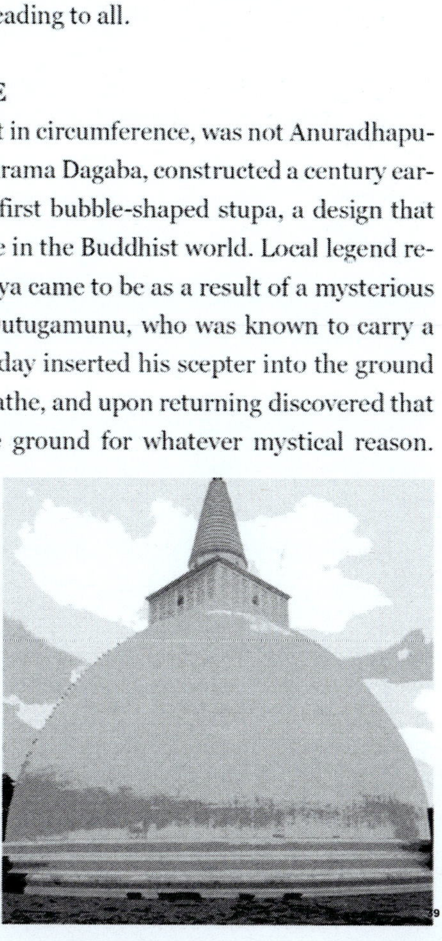

I stand alone in the presence of this

two-thousand-plus year-old structure that resembles the Ruanweli but in miniature form. A small section from the dome has been removed with surgical precision, cut out like a slice of cake revealing the crude brickwork within that render these structures as dense as they stand tall. Four cracked and misaligned brick altars around the dome face outward from the four cardinal directions, vines of ivy growing up through the cracks. Two summer clad European girls suddenly show up with several flustered Sinhalese in tow hollering about covering shoulders and sun-shorn skin while in the presence of the sacred site. We all three shrug at the infraction and the girls ask me to capture their photograph in front, to which I acquiesce.

Isurumuniya Rock Temple- 3rd Century BCE

While admiring the delicate etching on the boulderous façade of the Isurumuniya Rock Temple, a Buddhist monastery constructed like a fort into an array of erratic black boulders, a sudden deluge assaults the ancient city causing me to seek immediate shelter inside a nearby overly extravagant cave-temple. The inside is brightly colored but dimly lit. Buddha lies on his right side before me with his back against the wall. His head rests on his arm atop a pillow; his earlobes stretch nearly to his shoulders. He's at least thirty feet long. The bottoms of his feet appear a rich carmine-red and are propped on a pedestal resembling a large, dull red bottlecap, in front of which sits a "charity box." His dark red robe stops at his ankles and his skin looks jaundiceish. A mural covering the wall behind him depicts a number of *bikkhus* hovering in bluish clouds looking down admiringly as if from Heaven, their hands saintly clasped at their chests. Hard to imagine that when rediscovered by the British in the early 1800s this very cave was den to Sri Lanka's exotic sloth bears.

I exit this sensory-overload chamber as the rain ceases to pour and ascend twenty-three stone stairs framed by tombstone-like sidewings, each rendered identically depicting a Sinhalese guard posed beside two dwarf servants, the guard clad in a hood formed by a six-headed cobra. From atop the stairs a passageway weaves through the natural lie of giant ten-foot-tall rocks to a bodhi tree of medium height contained within a low gated enclosure, behind which stands a miniature white stupa — a child-size version. Opposite, crudes stairs chiseled into the rock zag narrowly through reddish slabs graffitied with directional Sinhala to a balcony peering out over the lush treescape eye level with the spire of a second, larger, on-site stupa, its copper steeple reflecting dull gray light. Several monks present gaze admiringly across the leafy expanse, their neonic orange robes in electrifying contrast to the landscape's saturated green foliage and pewter sky. To the west, clouds darken and descend and I can see a new curtain of rain pushing toward us across the level plain of Tissa Wewa.

Tissa Wewa- 3rd Century BCE

To ensure that the great city of Anuradhapura could sustain its large population of *bikkhus* (monks were forbidden by religious law to work and instead confined to accepting charity from the state), the ancient Sinhalese constructed a large-scale irrigation system reliant upon several immense manmade reservoirs (*wewas*). Lake Tissa, named after its great overseer King Devanampiyatissa (the same ruler who converted the ancient city into a Buddhist mecca), was merely one.

Measuring twelve miles in circumference and covering 550 acres, Lake Tissa maintains a maximum depth of 130-feet when full. Its front bund — essentially a dam — measures two miles long while rising 25-feet-high to the treetops. It seems unfathomable to me that a project this colossal was completed without the use of heavy machinery, but that is precisely the case — the closest the ancients had were elephants. And yet Tissa Wewa is just one of literally dozens of enormous watertanks that pock the island's landscape, including Nuwara Wewa, which covers five and a half times the surface area on the opposite side of town.

Following Anuradhapura's abandonment in the late 10th Century Tissa Wewa fell into disrepair. Erosive forces, however, failed to diminish its massive earthen bund. After the rain passes I scamper up its steep slope to where centuries-old banyans now grow and a newly paved pathway weaves a leisurely course for one to walk or pedal hither and tither.

Ranmasu Uyana- 2nd Century BCE

A short walk north along the bund of Tissa Wewa leads to Ranmasu Uyana (Gold Fish Park), a 40-acre "pleasure garden" that neighbors the Isurumuniya Rock Temple. In fact, Ranmasu Uyana incorporates into its lay the same array of erratic rocks that distinguish the Isurumuniya — smooth, dark slabs splayed across the landscape like natural slides, steps chiseled into them for convenient ascent and the ground between level with grass neatly trimmed.

Central to the Ranmasu Uyana is a deep multi-tiered stone pond (*pokuna*) that was at one time a public bath. It even retains a below-ground room built directly into the rocks that may have been a type of steam chamber. Sustainably, the water for this bath came directly from Tissa Wewa, and was afterward distributed as irrigation to the surrounding paddies. Meanwhile, upon a rockface nearby exists a curious cyclical petroglyph that some archeologists think an early attempt at a world map. Others think it is a sort of cosmological chart according to ancient Buddhist texts, and possibly the oldest known map of the universe.

NEW TOWN

Happy Swoon Rest

No A/C, no hot water, no tourists — no problem. Happy Swoon Rest resides discretely at the bottom of a dip in Old Bus Stand Road across from a modern Buddhist monastery where an authentic moonstone resides at the base of a stairway leading to an illuminated twenty-foot-tall statue of Buddha encased in glass. The Sri Lankan elder working the front desk lets me a room for a decent rate, complete with pink curtains and a pink mosquito net draped over a none-too-fancy bed containing only a pillow and bed sheet. No strings attached, no nasty paperwork to fill out. I simply pay up front and get the key. The bathroom window does not shut, monkeys peek in from outside, a man-eating cockroach shares floor space in the shower, and the walls I find pre-adorned with a number of evershifting geckos.

Sujeewa's Hotel

Come eveningtime I stop in Sujeewa's Hotel in central New Town for a late-night order of vegetable fried samba rice, a meal garnished with a fried chicken leg (or that of some fowl), a curious looking fish curry teeming with little bony anchovies, and a red jelly-like chutney preserving an ant. Despite the time of day I ingest my meal in a *rag*ing swelter not alleviated in the least by the clunky oscillating ceiling fan nor the pairs of eyes staring at me from the kitchen utterly bemused, like *What* are you doing in this greasy hotel at *this* time of night? Eventually, the owner, upon seeing the half-eaten meal yet to be embellished with the chutney/jelly condiment provided, takes it upon himself to *re*recommend it by dolloping several spoonfuls onto my plate, petrified ant included.

Nature Park

New Town's only public park, a two-square-block swath of undeveloped greenery, must also qualify as a veritable insect haven I have decided. Entering off Dharmapala Mawatha, I first encounter a life-size artificial statue *scene* depicting a man and woman dancing gaily in the jungle, a white dove perched symbolically on a branch above the woman's head while the man patriotically hoists the Sri Lankan national flag above the statue's artificial treetops. Some sad moat surrounds this scene, forcing me to cross a miniature gently-arching log bridge (also artificial). The whole ensemble looks like it's part of a child's backyard playset, or something found in a children's theme park.

Moving on, I am soon vividly reminded of the potential severity of the island's insect population when left unabated. Day or night, the epidemic is uniformly maddening, mosquitoes feasting painfully on exposed extremities while thousands of tiny gnats relentlessly swarm the head like something decomposing. It is no wonder these ancient cities were long plagued by malaria. Although I manage to tolerate the clouds of insects long enough to penetrate to the center of the park, I find only a barren gazebo populated by a number of bored primates not the least deterred by my sudden presence. As for the park's floral highlights, they are a testament to the true tenacity of the banyan tree (*ficus benghalensis*), that which lends credence to its rightful nickname: strangler fig. Again and again I see the lightish bark of the young banyan growing up through and around the darker bark of a much older variety of tree, like one snake swallowing another.

Carlten Restaurant

Just south of Nature Park, at the intersection of Maithripala Mawatha, above a small BOC (Bank of Ceylon) branch, I stumble upon the Carlten, a "Family Food" restaurant with an entrance down a narrow alley on the side of the building. Although the restaurant's name conjures European fare (I am think of Carlsberg beer, brewed in Denmark but widely distributed in Sri Lanka), the Carlten is most certainly an ethnic Sri Lankan bistro I discover after learning that half the menu is permanently "finish," meaning cannot be ordered. This means the Carlten no longer serves the majority of its menu, such as eastern and western Chinese fare, falafel, or cashew curry (which sounded great to me). "No have." Instead, I order the only selection not meat based: cabbage-heavy vegetable chop suey served on a bed of fried rice. The server in*sists* I season my meal with a customary red curry paste both delicious and dangerously spicy. And although no preserved insect is embedded in the condiment, I similarly exit looking like I have just stepped out of a sauna.

Railway Station

Signal boxes all along the rail line here are being re-painted glossy red to match the country's rail cars while men with backhoes hack into the ground long narrow canals for wire to be laid. Plus, the boarding platform is receiving its first hosing down in probably like a century, men concurrently sweeping away debris with tiny brooms. In fact, the entire Anuradhapura Railway Station is in full makeover mode in advanced preparation for the grand reopening of the Northern Line be*yond* Anuradhapura, to Kilinochchi, which will occur several weeks from now. But humans aren't the only ones hard at work. Anuradhapura's apes have descended upon the station and are exerting their presence as well, knocking over garbage cans, climbing the station rafters, hanging off the sideview mirrors of shiny motorbikes and using those bikes' seats as thrones — general hooliganism that only these primates can get away with. And there are dozens of them: young, old, male, female, mothers, babies clinging to the undersides of mothers like little parasites while mothers bound effortlessly from rail to tie to ledge to tree. What wonders they are! A reason in and of themselves to visit Anuradhapura.

7. Eastern Line

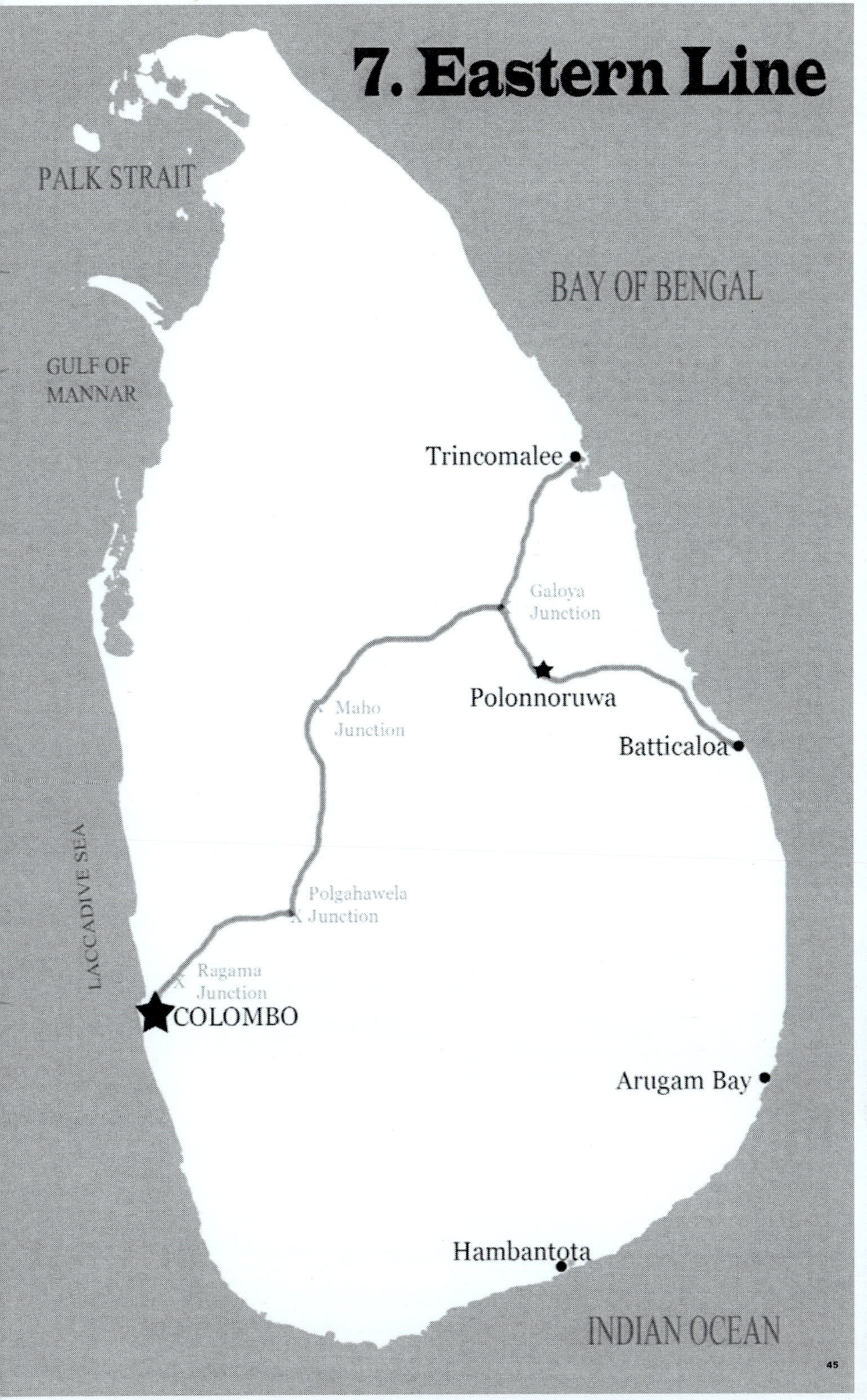

PART I: TRINCOMALEE LINE

Colombo ⇨ Trincomalee

2100- First Class on the Night Mail to Trincomalee — the only train to Trincomalee — is a kind of prison. I write this having never actually served time in prison, yet aboard the Night Mail it is feasible to imagine, or at least imagine what being transported while incarcerated is like. It is an overnight train clear across the island to the northeast coast — roughly 200 miles of low-grade track — and after departing Colombo I find myself locked in for the entire eight-hour run.

First Class, as it happens, is the only class of travel to afford the luxury of an assigned seat — not all Sri Lankan trains offer that — and not all trains off First Class. But since the Night Mail *did* offer First Class (it is an overnight train after all) I waited in line inside a stuffy room at Colombo Fort Railway Station for two hours the day before in order to pre-purchase a ticket. What I ended up purchasing was a ticket for a sleeper-car, which not even in the States when riding Amtrak have I been able to afford the luxury of private sleeper Yet upon boarding the Night Mail I suddenly found myself being ushered into a seven-foot by five-foot cell of a room complete with a dingy metal sink (like found in a prison cell), a rickety ceiling fan circulating hot air, bunks that folded down from the wall, and a shared lavatory (also dingy metal) connecting to the adjacent cell of a room.

At first I was alone, but shortly before departure a thirty-some-odd-year-old in a striped polo entered to claim the bottom bunk and my experience became less like solitary confinement. I laid the top bunk (I would have selected the bottom had I known how miserably stuffy the room would become once the door was shut), and as the train departed the ceiling fan, a few feet from my face and sounding like a gigantic buzzing fly, began to oscillate slightly. There being no windows in the cell, this oscillation became the only real indicator of the train's movement.

Soon a ticket agent came through to inspect tickets; once this was done my cellmate shut the door and turned out the light, which concurrently shut off the buzzing fan, causing quite a swelter build up inside the room. Feeling more claustrophobic than tired, I freed myself temporarily in the diaphragm between cars and seated myself on a little fold-down seat probably designed for the ticket agent and finished off a pint of Harrier whisky (cheap, Sri Lankan quality). As the train sped on, slowing considerably every four or five minutes but never quite stopping, I could see nothing on the outside the car except for the occasional blurring-by light. The sleeper cells were all full up; none more boarded. Only the occasional Dopplered blaring by of passing trains gave indication of our own progress.

*

0530- There is something extremely comforting about being rocked to sleep aboard a moving train. The orchestral rhythms, cadences, and innumerable noises sounding invisibly from under and around the bosom of the beast can be inoculating. This morning, despite the sleeper car feeling like a prison cell complete with an unfamiliar cellmate, I wished the ticket agent would have let us First Class passengers sleep a little longer. After all, the train was not going anywhere right away. Reality, though, was not too out of line with the rude awakening that comes with life in a jail cell: Get up, you're getting out!

Outside, the dawn Trincomalee sky possessed just enough cloudcover to obscure the direction from which the sun was beginning to rise, and in my half-asleep state I had difficulty discerning which direction to attend to, which was actually just fine with me since I prefer to arrive to new places with only a mental map of the area's general geography and terrain. Where but for the grace of the Elephant God go I, into stranger and stranger lands, where things never do present themselves as I imagined them but where I always manage to find my way.

Continuing upon the trajectory the train tracks had intended, I arrived at a muted shoreline. Colorful, cracked facades crammed in tightly around the sand, cut through by alleys decorated with tangles of wires atop concrete electrical poles. Catamarans of excessive vividness lined the rust-colored shore before me, where fishermen went unnoticingly about their morning routines while their wives and children remained whisperly quiet, as if frightened by my specter. As I crossed the sand toward the water the more proximal stray dogs awakened to the presence in measured movements.

The body of water before me, while no doubt oceanic, also appeared far too calm and *un*ocean-like to convince me of my definitive location. Then it occurred to me suddenly, like an epiphany in my early morning daze: no longer was I on the west coast of the island where for the past month and a half I have watched the sun set below monsoon rains rolling in. I had been overnighted clear across the island to its *east* coast where the sun will in fact now rise *from* the sea instead of setting upon it. I then turned to perceive the sun emerging not on the horizon before me or the train station behind but from a pinnacle of rock to my right. Ahead I marched toward the sun's ascending glare, following a vacant strip of pavement lined with empty lots and cricket-worn fields, eventually arriving at the enormous telltale stone walls of a colonial-era citadel surrounded by rocks and sea in front.

Notes From Trincomalee

Day 1

- Dutch Bay: the serenity entrancing. placidity unexpected (wholly). water clear and cool, lapping gently on the concave contour of sand like not really the sea at all. shore steep — abrupt — like worn away by rising sea levels. wooden catamarans and dorys painted in striking primary colors line the sand. embossed palms poke out from between one- and two-story houses. dogs lie on the sand in the shade while a group of weathered, dark-skinned fishermen haul in a large buoyed net, slowly. they form two lines of 5 spread apart about like 40 yds. each line rotating — last guy to the front, and so on. the guy in front grips the emerging trawl (cyclic) and reties it and passes it back to the next guy, over and over, hands gripping and feet backpedaling as if tugging along an inert automobile. the two lines are no doubt tugging two sides of the same trawl that will eventually emerge between them filled with whatever sand-covered marine life they've managed to scrape from the sea floor.

- Dutch Bay faces ESE into the Bay of Bengal on a boot-shaped peninsula along the island's NE shore that comprises the N shore of greater Trincomalee Bay. It's called Dutch Bay cause it is where the Dutch landed in 1650-something to overtake the adjacent fort here that was constructed by and then occupied by the Portuguese. (prev labeled on a 1762 map as /"Baye des Hollondais."/) (Trinco was /"Trinquemalay."/)

- while sitting with my back against a dory, writing, 2 tourists (can't escape them) emerge from the backdoor of a shoreside guest house — a couple, the girl with dyed blonde hair, wearing a bikini. they dive into the water and last like 3 mins before the girl complains that something crawled across her arm, or that she felt something on her arm, and maybe it stung her. both retreat back into the guest house and are not seen again.

- the ocean appears a calming spa-water-looking teal and behaves gently — I can't overemphasize that. what little waves it produces curl at the shore and explode subtly — no crashing — onto the sand with that soothing rainstick-like sound that starts out loud and strong but filters away rapidly. it's a scene remarkably serene yet not as pure as it 1st looks. sewage from the town and nearby neighborhood — dark gray and putrid smelling — drains dir into the bay at like 3 or 4 diff places. houses even have plastic piping running beneath the sand and discharging dir into the sea. no water treatment whatsoever. open sewers. crows love it. (cows don't mind it either.)

• 2 black-crow-looking ducks (they have long necks) soar down and land in front of me on the water and immed dive under, and after like 2 or 3 secs beneath the surface an entire school of little fishies come leaping up out of the water like tiny dolphins, the ducks re-emerging after them. the fish then just keep jumping, trying to escape being lunch. it's like something from a Nat Geo video — so delicate and phenomenal; I can hardly believe it just happened so casually before my eyes here on this battered seashore midday.

• Trincomalee Bay = the fifth largest natural harbor in the world, and a natural deep-sea harbor at that. it is vast and scenic and slightly hilly at points, like the San Francisco Bay pre-Golden Gate Bridge — pre-Gold Rush, pre-discovery even. imagine the SF Bay: same size and scope, yet the land surrounding sparsely developed except for just the peninsula of land where SF now exists, and only developed minimally — that's Trincomalee (the town of course is much narrower in width), and Trinco Bay is by far the largest bay on the island. alas, it also the least significant. ships just don't use it as a port any more.

• the reverse opposite of Dutch Bay (W side of the town) is "Inner Harbour," and is literally the opposite of D Bay, meaning windy and cold (almost) and a true tragedy of the commons. strong winds from the west rake in carbuncle water strewn with colored plastic (bags, cups, wrappers) driftwood, fishing nets, tangles of used line, etc etc, accompanied by a pervasive stench. meanwhile, one part of the bay is so severely receded it looks like the low tide at a high declination locale (like in Maine). a good-sized boat, half-capsized, pierces the exposed mud. a minor road mirrors the shore — boulder enforced and relatively clean and newly paved. down on the rocks a man bundles driftwood and ties these bundles with pieces of net gleaned from among the rocks. far off in the water stands a metropolistic oil-rig-looking structure used for loading and unloading container ships that looks abandoned. only a couple small(er) ships (possibly tugboats) sit anchored at bay.

• while walking along the Inner Harbour road I nearly step on a pointy gastropod, a shell delicate and fragile like you'd see in some natural history museum, or sold in a touristy souvenir shop. it's about the length of my index finger and not very wide, and still dirty inside from its former inhabitant. western tourists comb remote beaches for these souvenirs and here one is in dirty Trincomalee unaccounted for on the filthy Inner Harbour shore sidewalk. (I imagine it got here by a gull snatching it up and devouring the mollusk inside and then letting fall the shell, or perhaps just setting it down after eating the housed mollusk.)

• to the north of Dutch Bay, opposite the fort, is Back Bay (facing GEO NE into the sea). this is where I found myself this morning greeted by unintimidating strays. the place now reveals itself to be not so pristine either, nor any more welcoming in the afternoon hours. the glistening wet sand appears pewter from dirty sewage and the water not clear. meanwhile, strays remain territorial. one bark sets off a chain reaction of other barks that correspond approx to my movement. yet no stray strays far from its personal territory: they simply pass me off to the next timid canine.

• separating Back Bay from Dutch Bay is a forested arm of land jutting eastward into the sea like the spur of a boot heal. here stands nearly-four-hundred-year-old Fort Frederick, started by the Dutch in the early 1600s, finished by the Portuguese, capitulated and re-fortified by the Dutch, later briefly held by the French, taken /back/ by the Dutch, then controlled by the British until the island came into its own after WWII. its outer stone and mortar ramparts rise mossily from the ground at characteristically slightly inward canted angles. bushes sprout horizontally out of cracks. a thick archway with still-attached wooden doors marks the entrance while an elaborate Dutch Shield hanging overhead reads: ANNO 1675. enter: barracks and various military dealingswith now occupied by the SL Army. a shady road winds past several buildings and a couple of military-run cafes/hutches, one of which I patronize for a desp needed bottle of agua. a colonial white mansion that looks like some old slave-master quarters, sits slightly back from the road behind an e/nor/mous banyan with sprawling-out branches and aerial roots stalactiting into the earth. banyans, when you are able to stand back and really observe them in their totality, are just re/mark/able organisms.

• the highest point in all of Trinco, just past Fort Fred, contains on it an old Hindu temple. this great rock outcropping — Swami Rock — is said to have been a pilgrimage site for Hindus since BCE (east side of the island = predom Tamil; Tamils = predom Hindu). the name Trincomalee is in reference to this "sacred" rock feature and is said to mean (possibly) "sacred eastern hill." the cliff is nearly four-hundred-feet high and drops directly into the sea. supposedly during Dutch times a young girl leapt suicidally from the cliff in grief over an estranged love, which gives it its modern-day colloquial nom de plume: "Lovers Leap."

• walking up the steep road to Swami Rock I am able to look out (N) across the full splay of Back Bay, a dimple in the amalgam of smaller bays and harbors that comprise the enorm bay of Trinco, and it is much more picturesque from above.

• most interesting: right where the road splits up toward Swami (to the left) and toward a large cellular antenna that is off limits to the public (right) is a lush shady patch of foliage where huge #s of spotted deer (bucks, does, fawns) lie content together, all /not/ scattering at the presence of a human (their sheer numerosity is like a source of camouflage in itself). a sign posted at the fort's entrance addresses their delicate existence (they are known to have resided here since at least the 17th C when this fort was built, but likely their pop dates back into the times of the ancients). I've never witnessed anything in nature to this degree of docility. it almost feels zooish.

• back in the Dutch Bay neighborhood streets little children holler /"Hallow!"/ at me as I walk past. most people are friendly, but some young hotel hosts have seemed outright predatory so from their places I've stayed away.

• Lion Strong can be found on tap at the Trinco Village, a tiki-style restaurant that locals abuse like a bar. it is the only beer on tap, which is astounding and /wrong/. this would be like going to a semi-nice restaurant in the States with servers and all and finding the only beer on draught to be Steel Reserve, Colt 45, Mad Dog — name your poison. (only 130 rs a glass though!)

Day 2

• I found a relatively cheap (2,000 rs) room in a small guest house run by an old man and his young son on a st. called Dyke. the back-patio's door opens to the pristine golden sand and remarkably placid crystalclear Dutch Bay water. a stray cat hangs around the patio (roofless) with one of its (I assume) kittens, and a stray pit-bull-looking mutt loiters timidly inside, too. as soon as I noticed the dog the owner-man shooed it away saying it belonged outside. its name is Sticks (the man said). the dog lets me pet it. it lies on the warm sand at my feet while I sit out back and write. things here can be so tranquil and perfect it's hard to imagine it's had any violent or contested history in the past.

• last night after dark, whilst walking along the tide's edge, I noticed a huge trawl floating in the water close to shore, visible in moonlight. what was its purpose? I wondered. fishing is the locals' livelihood and I couldn't understand why a huge net could be left to drift out to sea. the trawl seemed to just hover — not sinking or surfacing — just floating in the water, ebbing and flowing gently with the tide. I entertained myself for a time by zoomorphing it a huge blood-red jellyfish washed to shore, or a gigantic 6-ft-wide stingray hovering sleepily above the sand. my interest grew as I waded out into the water thinking I could drag it back ashore and in doing so do some fisherman a favor. but when I neared the thing I could scarcely believe what was before me — alive indeed, yet no singular organism at all. astoundingly, it was a dark dense shoal of fish, impossibly numerous, rotating rapidly, like a time-lapse galaxy, sparkling and flittering in the moonlight. the revolving mass ebbed and flowed in tandem with the gentle tide, yet the fish — I suppose asleep — were somehow still subconsciously aware of each others' presence and uniform movement so as not to collide, as well as external bodies (mine) enough that when the tide washed the shoal near my shins the entire mass instinctively divided into two like by magnetic repulsive force, each ,amazingly, maintaining the same apparent size as before.

Day 3

• I have been sitting outside this hotel all day like a stoner drinking 7-up and ginger cola (the cola's OK in this country 'cause it's made w/ cane sugar and not corn syrup). something yesterday got me very ill. it could have been the dhal and rice and paratha I had for lunch/late-breakfast at the Muslim guy's hotel on the corner; could've been the greasy vegi fried rice I ate later in the day that served as my dinner, or the bootlegged bottle of fermented toddy with no label that I bought off some guy on the street outside the wine shop for only 90 rupees and that even tho I had doubts about its purity drank (and enjoyed). Whatever, on top of that I think I developed mild heat-stroke after walking around so much yest (I had difficulty keeping hydrated 'cause water here so quickly loses its "coolness" that it doesn't affect my system in the same hydrational way, it seems). The night passed insufferably. first came the aches: so severe they caused me to contort my body in extreme ways to relieve them. my room was stuffy and hot and not alleviated by the fan, and I ran out of water to drink (wouldn't dare drink from the bathroom-sink tap when already so ill). then came the stomach cramps, followed by an early-A.M. blasting of diarrhea so severe I wondered had I ever experienced anything so truly wretched. a fever ensued. I was compelled to stand under the cold shower to cool myself (no hot water anyway), and then lay down under a weak ceiling fan blowing down hot air. this morning I had little energy. my urine was a dark yellow (almost orange) and smelled noxious. I have no appetite or desire to eat. after lying in bed for hours I am still aching.

• today is Poya but no huge celebration is happening in Trinco a sweet girl at a small pharmacy where I went for medicine told me. she gave me 5 capsules that look like something out of a Dr Mario game and said to take one a day for 5 days, then laughed when I asked about Poya and said that big Poya fests were for Buddhist mainly. I suppose she's Tamil, and therefore Hindu (as the vast majority of Trinco goes).

• tonight, many are out and about the beach of Dutch Bay for moonrise, in-

cluding very many Muslim women dressed in trad black garb. families "bathe" in the placid water, the waning sunlight gloaming off the sea and sand turning everything pink. some of the men are shirtless in shorts, but most swim in their everyday clothes. SL women do not wear bathing suits — they swim in their normal clothes; yet still somehow their clothes always appear spotless and clean. no one minds the cows that share the sand with them either. (are cows still considered sacred to Hindus?)

Trincomalee ⇨ Galoya Jct

1300- No train runs directly to Batticaloa from Trincomalee. In order to get to Batticaloa by train one must first backtrack to Galoya and there board an entirely new, Batticaloa-bound train. I know nothing about Galoya other than it is a tri-directional (northeast/southeast/west) junction located 45 miles inland in a sparsely inhabited very arid region. However, since a mid-afternoon train *does* run to Galoya from Trincomalee I assume a same-day connection to Batticaloa can be made, or at least a connection to Polonnaruwa, which is on the way to Batticaloa and attracts many tourists. Otherwise, what sense would there be in running a mid-afternoon train? But now, as the train departs and I see that I am the *only* passenger aboard, I realize I may have been making false assumptions.

Four cars total comprise this mid-afternoon train: an engine (a basic low-horsepower yard unit) manned by an able-bodied engineer, two third-class coach cars of which I am the sole passenger, and a caboose on the rear carrying mail and the conductor/brakeman. These are old, wooden cars — creaky and splintery and painted solid maroon on the outside. I am seated on a bench along the wall of the first coach car and when the engine's horn blares it does so with headachingly loud proximity due to there being no doors on the car and all windows open. On Sri Lankan trains this fresh air effect is perpetual. Only maybe if it's downpouring will you ever find a train car's windows shut (and the vast majority of trains don't have doors), and that would still have to be left to passenger initiative.

Leaving Trincomalee behind, the train skirts north around the bay, climbing slightly in elevation through the town of China Bay, which forms the backside shore of Trincomalee's polluted Inner Harbor. Beyond China Bay the train follows the north shore of Tambalagam Bay, a smaller, more inland bay that is still part of greater Trincomalee Bay. Here, the water appears shallow and muddy; light blue dories and splinters of blue dories float solemnly near the shore.

Once entirely free of Trincomalee's gravitational pull, the land reverts to low, arid, and largely nondescript save for gently rising hills in the northern distance. The tracks ahead, straight as an arrow in their intended direction, undulate noticeably. Beneath, crossties alternate between old rotting wood and new, slightly bowed concrete. It's like the tracks were upgraded recently, but with only every third tie replaced. Burnt *chenas* blur past, along with slender concrete electrical poles carrying a single wire. Halfway to our destination, in Kantale, I glimpse the bund of a 4,700-acre reservoir dug out of the earth.

*

1450- Galoya Junction is really out there as far as train stations go, and not a part of any municipality whatsoever. Other than an amenityless train station, Galoya consists of only a tiny market on a hill. That is all.

In front of the tiny market sit twenty or so men eating rice and curry with their hands. I enter and purchase two large bottles of water (I was beginning to dehy-

drate aboard the train), then return to the station and sit in the shade where it is oddly cool and windy. Surrounding me are some of the homeliest, most pathetic looking stray dogs, hackneyed breeds lying in the shade beneath idle train cars. Men work around them using handheld tools — wrenches, sledgehammers, bolt-tighteners, crowbars — working in their everyday clothes — sarongs or slacks and sandals — like you would never see in the States due to all sorts of liabilities, requirements, and regulations. Based solely on appearance there's no telling if a rail worker is a career employee or some *arrack*aholic pulled from the gutter to perform non-contractual day-labor. I watch curiously as two men complete a section of track work, carry their big metallic wrenches over to a nearby water spigot, and commence to clean the tools using bar soap and jungle vines. After rinsing the tools a homely old dog with rampant mange visits the soapy oily refuse for a quick drink.

Turns out there's not a train to Batticaloa until around midnight, and the next one after that's not until tomorrow morning at nine A.M. This presents a quandary for me because there is virtually no place here for me to stay other than with the leeches. (Why does a mid-afternoon train run to Galoya from Trincomalee when there is not a connecting train, and when no one rides the train anyway?) A station worker tells me that I am welcome to sleep at the station until the midnight train arrives, and at that points to the "Gentlemen's Waiting Room," a small open room off to the side of the stenchably noteworthy "Toilet Room." The waiting room is currently full of on-break railway workers sprawled out on benches and lying supine on bare wooden tables — the same crew who were just minutes ago eating rice and curry with their hands outside the little market up the hill.

The offer is tempting — the colorful characters I would meet I could not otherwise imagine, I'm sure — but I would be extremely uncomfortable, not to mention unable to rest due to the flies. I walk to the far end of the station and sit on a bench to think over what to do, meanwhile trying to make the acquaintance of some homely bitch (however, no dog will come near me.)

In the States this'd be no problem, I could pass the time reading or writing, lounging by the tracks, a lake or river, or take a bus to some small town new to me. But this is not America. There are no buses out here. There's not even a drivable road nearby and I haven't seen or heard a tuk-tuk in hours (which is a bit unsettling). Besides, the flies about the station are an absolute scourge to the extent that I do not know how the workers can even perform the labor that they do, and leeches probably proliferate in the surrounding jungle. Plus, just coming off a wrenching sickness, I feel dangerously susceptible to everything I eat and drink, and so of course I am majorly concerned about what I will eat and drink here during the next twenty hours, which is how long I'd end up waiting since I would not bother to board the midnight train just to get dumped in Polonnaruwa (where I intend to go next) a couple of hours later (at 2 A.M. nonetheless). After all, my intention is to ride these trains in the daytime if possible (which it is). That said, my decision manifests as the only truly logical one for me: return to Trincomalee and set out again at dawn in order to return to Galoya Junction in time to make the 9 A.M. connection to Polonnaruwa.

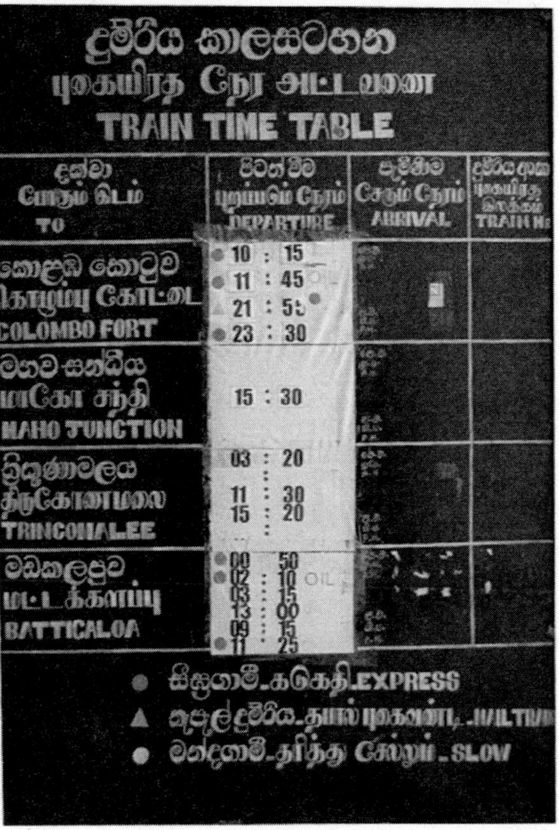

Galoya Jct. ⇨ **Trincomalee**

1700- My return to Trincomalee takes place aboard the very same train I traveled to Galoya on, and is nearly as deserted except for a couple of elderly women carrying baskets of clothes. My first thought of an alternative plan is to get off at China Bay, one station stop from Trincomalee. Earlier I had spotted an active little train yard there and I can easily imagine myself probing around it after dark. But as the trip progresses I think of a different option: Kantale, the only significant town along the way. I consider Kantale because schedulewise it would be more ideal and afford me an extra hour in the morning. The only problem is, I don't know if Kantale will have any place for me to stay either. What I *do* know is that I'm on the last train back to Trincomalee and I don't want to get stranded anywhere. But then, when the train arrives in Kantale and I see how *truly* remote the town is (despite a young family getting off there), I safe guess myself and stay on board.

The final stretch of the return trip proves an equally scenic journey in alternate light, and with more families aboard (mostly mothers and sleeping children). For my part, I stare raptly into the sparse fringe jungle — a bucolic refuge for endangered wildlife — keeping watch for the snouty foraging of the reclusive sloth-bear (found only in SE

Asia), wild rummaging tuskers, or a glimpse of the ever elusive spotted leopard (*panthera pardus kotiya*), a sub-species unique to Sri Lanka. All I spot though are an abundance of tree-inhabiting monkeys transferring effortlessly from branch to branch amid the flutters and chirps of unidentifiable avian.

Upon arriving in China Bay the engine detaches off a couple "goods cars" it has been carrying and backs them into the yard. With the extra time allotted I step off the train and inquire to a man standing nearby (most likely a driver) about a rest house to stay at. No rest houses in China Bay, the man tells me. No good rest houses in Trincomalee either. The man then pulls a business card from his front shirt pocket and hands it to me. It reads: Hotel Oshin (play on words or bad translation?). The ocean hotel sounds nice — a beachside room somewhere north of Trincomalee where I've heard the beaches are pretty. Plus, I could use a relaxing day after this long day of redundant travel. However, I cannot tell from the business card if the place will be too high-class for me, and I want to be careful not to put myself in a compromising situation where I'm forced to spend more than I can afford simply because it is late in the day and I am too worn-down to look elsewhere. To this dilemma, I ask the man to call and inquire about a single-room rate for me. He hands me his phone instead.

"You call," I tell him, "*You* speak the language."

He blushes, walks over to another driver, and asks that driver to dial for him the numbers.

Unfortunately, Sri Lankan telecodes can be far more complicated than need be, especially now that most people use cell phones. Repeatedly the tuk-tuk driver can't get through to the ocean hotel, or perhaps he isn't dialing the number correctly. Regardless, the train airs up to depart and I am left with no choice but to hop back on board.

And so it goes. But not to worry, I've been thinking about a curious sign I saw earlier at the Trinco railway station, and I decide that when I arrive I

will inquire to it.

*

1850- A stocky man with a glabrous head and a thick mustache cannot grasp what I am asking so I lead him to the lobby of the station and point to a small hanging sign that reads: RETIRING ROOMS ARE AVILABLE [sic] AT THIS RAILWAY STATION.

"You want room?"

He finally understands me but reports that the retiring rooms at the station are "broken," all of them, apparently. Alas, it is an outdated sign, likely from the 60s or 70s. However, being as how it is late, the man senses he can be of some assistance to me and informs me of a nearby "crew quarters." Although, he adds, it may not be at all what I'm looking for.

The man is the station porter, he says, taking out his antiquated flip-phone to call the engineer ("He is driver of train!"), the same engineer it turns out who just ran the train to *and* from Galoya (and who I noticed *did* save several bovine lives on the return). Moments later the engineer walks over. He is dressed semi-professionally in khaki slacks and a stainless peach polo. He is tall, in his mid-forties with a rounded belly, and has grinning white teeth to go with a pleasant smile. Smiling, he hands the porter a set of keys. I then follow the porter across the street to a boarded-up-looking one-story white house. The porter unlocks the front door and we enter a large, mostly barren front room with two doors on either side and a doorway straight-ahead leading to a back area. The room on the left contains a bed with a long mosquito net draped over it and random personal belongings strewn around on the floor. At the foot of the bed stands a not-plugged-in oscillating fan and near a window sits a small desk. This, the porter tells me, is where the engineer sleeps. The room on the right is less cluttered but no larger and has two beds, both with mosquito nets, but no fan. It is a stuffy room, the bedspreads stained and dirty, the mattresses sagging. The porter asks if I have my own bedding with me, which I do, to which he remarks "one night then no problem."

I really can't gauge the appropriateness of my accepting the railway crew-quarters being offered, but instinctively I'm inclined not to. However, in a country where customs and expectations differ vastly from my own (not to mention the remarkable language barrier hindering me), I find myself unable to initially decline. To be honest, I don't really like the porter. He comes across as boisterous, a late-night arrack drunk with red betel stains coating his teeth. I'm not saying I'm afraid of him, but I do sense in him a genuine shyster and I do not want to subject myself to another I-help-you-now-you-help-me *quid pro quo* soon-to-turn-into-a-morose-declamation-of-personal-misery-preluding-an-uncalled-for-homoerotic-advance type of situation. Yet still, the porter *is* going out of his way to help me, and I do not want to come across as ungrateful. On the other hand, I do like the engineer, and the crew-quarters *would* be insightful not to mention most practical; besides, the room probably wouldn't cost more than a bottle of cheap arrack, if anything.

Thanking the porter without formally accepting the offer, I leave my pack in the second bedroom and tell him I am going into town in search of a bite to eat before everything closes. In reality, I plan to find another place along the way and then return to retrieve my bag.

*

1930- One thing you never see in Sri Lanka — never (and I did encounter a female tuk-tuk driver in Nawalapitiya so it's not that) — one thing you never see are women purchasing or drinking alcohol — I mean *never*. Yet as far as I know there is no law banning the consumption of alcohol by women (nor some blanket religious tenet prohibiting alcohol consumption that doesn't apply to men). Still, Sri Lankan towns after dark tend to be very homogeneous, almost to a fault. Not entirely, but very. Downtown Trincomalee appears no exception.

The King's Restaurant, the first place I come to where I consider dining, is but a crowded smoky bar slash liquor store where men actively bid on fifths of arrack and tall-cans of malt liquor. Upstairs (technically the "restaurant" part) resembles yet another dive bar. The scene is most depressing: every table taken by one or two Sri Lankan men, a full pint or empty glass in front of them and half the men with their heads down, face in their hands. Pale smoke hangs in the air, and a cacophony of noises reverberates from above, below, and beyond. No one even looks up to notice me standing in the doorway, which happens to be to my benefit because I have no desire to stay. Upon exiting I encounter a beguiling sign posted near the entrance that in my mind remains the only redeeming aspect to the place. It reads: "Not Aloud Liquor And Bite Bring From Outside."

I wander tenuously down the chaos of the main street and fortunately find a small hotel still serving food. It is the only other eatery I find open. The man behind the counter greets me warmly. On the countertop beneath a pane of thick glass upon which sits the register is a collection of global paper currency, including a one dollar bill that I find myself taking odd mental comfort in. It's been a long time since I've seen old George.

After placing my normal order the owner brings me several vegetarian curries and cold paratha, then replenishes each as I consume them. At one point, he presents to me a dark curry and asks if I like expressy.

"Expressy?" I inquire. "What is *Expressy?*"

I can tell by looking that the curry type is soya (a cheap meat substitute popular on the island), and so I try it. As soon as I do I know what he was trying to ask: do I like spicy.

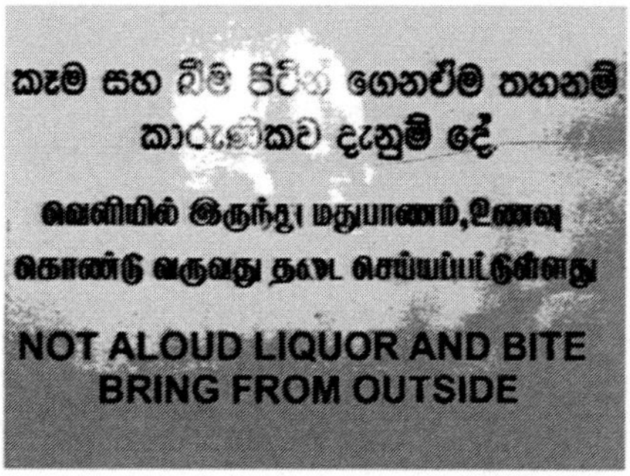

What I have come to realize, finally, is that Sri Lankan hotel food — spicy or not — generally upsets my stomach, still, especially when the food is served lukewarm, which unfortunately, I find myself prone to eating more often than not while too timorous to rescind the order or ask for something other, especially at night when I know of little else open. (Of course this makes sense considering the one species on the island capable of perpetually outnumbering the Sinhalese are its flies.) The trick, I've found, is to eat just enough to satiate my hunger and no more, and to this tenet I now adhere strictly.

As I walk back to the crew quarters following my meal I resolve to tell the porter and engineer that I have found a room down the street, even though I have not. In all honesty, I feel too tired to socially interact anymore today and I'd rather sleep outdoors in the Trincomalee train yard just to be alone. Besides, it's a clear starry night, and as far as I know leeches do not persist along the coast.

*

2100- The moon, tonight almost full, sits low on the horizon above the train yard. Melodies and voices drift across the open expanse of mostly empty tracks like scents in the breeze. On the shore of Back Bay an open-door mass fills the air with liturgy. Further distant, the acappellic chants of Muslim prayer hour can be discerned faintly, blending ominously with the sounds of the Christian ritual.

I enter the yard unobstructed and locate away from the station a short, shallow open-top gondola, a car used primarily to transport railroad ties and ballast. The car is empty and appears relatively clean inside. I decide it the perfect bed on which to spend my first night in the Sri Lankan outdoors. But first I need to find some sort of insulation from the cold surface steel on which I plan to sleep. I return to the station to search for a piece of cardboard and in doing so inadvertently run into the porter walking briskly toward me five steps ahead of the engineer. Both have been anxiously awaiting my re-arrival in order to turn in for the night themselves.

The engineer, now firmly in control of the situation, says for me to follow him. As he walks confidently past toward the crew quarters I almost — *almost* — inform the porter about changing my mind, but before I am able to the porter climbs into a tuk-tuk and rattles off muttering about arrack. I have no choice but to follow the engineer to the house, and I do so mustering the courage to disappoint him.

When I arrive at the house the engineer holds the front door for me enter, beaming. He seems unnaturally proud, as if he is genuinely opening up his home to me; unlike the porter his smile feels authentic and just *warm.* Pure graciousness and geniality exude from the man, and try as I might I just cannot bring myself to disappoint him now. He leads me to the room the porter earlier told me was the engineer's. The bed has been cleared and has new sheets on it. He points to a desk against the wall, an object of luxury here, then plugs in the fan and turns it on and tells me I can open the window for fresh air if I please. He then leaves and I am alone, and relieved to be. Aside from the persistent fear that I may miss the 7 A.M. departure and find myself stuck in this whole ordeal again, I must acknowledge how comfortable I am, and relaxed, and this is entirely due the Good Samaritanism of the station porter and train engineer. The Sri Lankan people, I'm glad to know, are not as distrustful as I have at times feared.

Trincomalee ⇨ Galoya Jct

0700- I am awakened at six by a sharp rapping on the door (although I'm already half awake), and open the door to the engineer, his face still beaming.

"Wash face," he says, indicating what he means with simultaneous clockwise and counter-clockwise scrubbing motions made with his hands. In the back room I find a sink and a dish with bar soap. I wash my face, brush my teeth, and return to the room and pack my things. On my way out of the house I hand the engineer 1,000 rupees and tell him I appreciate the hospitality. I don't know if he'll take my money but with a show of pride equal to that of his harboring me he pockets it, and I'm glad he does.

At the railway station I purchase a little breakfast at a cafeteria called The Canteen (black coffee no sugar, and a pastry resembling a muffin), then immediately board the train. A minute later we depart.

The train car is again totally empty until two young girls board in Kantale along with their mother and father and grandmother. Interestingly, the girls choose to sit in the same booth as I, facing me, while their parents remain across the aisle. The girls are close in age, undoubtedly sisters, and both inherently Sri Lankanly beautiful — strong jawed and with smooth, flawless chicory skin and straight, jet-black hair. They are pleasant to oppose and to watch interact, and I appreciate their adolescent courage: for once I feel not the pariah of the train who only drunken men and hubristic teenage boys take notice of. At a station stop along the way, when the rollicking noise of the train momentarily ceases, the younger sister disturbs my writing and bravely speaks.

"What is your name," she asks carefully.

She responds that hers is Dushani (or some variation of spelling), and that they, the family, are traveling to Anuradhapura. I, in turn, must show her on my little atlas where I am heading because my accent must be butchering the native Polonnaruwa.

PART II: BATTICALOA LINE

Galoya Jct. ⇨ Polonnaruwa

0900- Arriving in Galoya, I bid farewell to the two sisters and hurry across the platform at the front end of the station (instead of exiting properly like everyone else) and board directly onto what I assume is a Batticaloa-bound train. Once aboard I notice the train to be sparsely crowded, about *as* crowded as the train *from* Trincomalee was. Meanwhile no one from the train I arrived on boards. Instead, everyone remains seated on benches outside the station, waiting. It's odd. *Why don't others board? What train are* they *waiting for?* Then, before any announcement is made designating the train, without warning and before anyone else can board, off we go. I keep expecting the train to stop, reverse onto a different track, and return to pick up the rest of the passengers, but that never happens (and of course I make certain I'm not just headed back to Trincomalee). Once the train passes the Mineriya Tank, an ancient reservoir surrounded by BCE ruins, I no longer have any doubt where it's destined and seat myself in an available seat to await my next stop: the medieval capital Polonnaruwa.

Polonnaruwa

The Polonnaruwa Railway Station actually resides in Kaduruwela, a busy little stretch of Muslim influenced road four kilometers from Polonnaruwa. Here, a number of ostentatious trishaw drivers duly await daily train arrivals. I have no trouble enlisting the services of one such driver standing saronged outside the fray. He silently obliges my request and off we go.

I do not have prior reservations in Polonnaruwa, therefore I rely on the Polonnaruwa Rest House as my default drop-off location, although I do not know if such a rest house even exists. Turns out the Polonnaruwa Rest House *does* exist, yet it proves to be in such a condition as to be considered it*self* ruinous. Nevertheless, the driver drops me in front of the out-of-service rest house atop the steep bund of a body of water larger than most of the island's lagoons, bays, towns — even cities. This vast watery expanse, actually an aggregate of multiple earthen reservoirs, is known as the Parakrama Samudra (Sea of Parakrama) and covers more than nine square-miles with a maximum depth of 52 feet (when full). Far-off, mountains dot the horizon, while from the surface of the water jet-streams a battering wind. Naturally, I am caused to wonder: were the ancient Sinhalese, if not impressively advanced enough by the time they established Polonnaruwa, actually on the verge of discovering their own source of renewable energy by means of generating wind? and if so how would that discovery have altered the course of not only 10th Century Polonnaruwa's history but the longevity of the Sinhalese Kingdom as a whole?

My ruminations, however, are abruptly disrupted, for the Parakrama Samudra today, with a leisurely walking / biking path laid atop its bund, happens to be fiercely patrolled by a tuk-tuk driver / guest-house owner by the name of Bandula, who upon spotting me under the burden of my luggage mandatorily detours over to aggressively touts his services, despite his already harboring a passenger. He himself matter-of-factly and hands me his business with such assertion that it feels like he is serving me divorce papers. Since I expect to find accommodations in Polonnaruwa somewhere in the 2,000 to 2,500 rupee range I tactically lowball the mercenary, offering him 1,500 rupees for a room, hoping that he'll leave me alone. He does, eventually (he has a passenger to attend to, after all), and in his immediate absence I follow into town a wide shallow sluice channel. In its slime-green water amid an abundance of overripe palmyra fruit sulks monitor lizard the size of a damn crocodile. I quickly snap a few pictures before the creature disappears slowly, almost robotically, back into its sewer hole of a home; as I am doing this the tuk-tuk driven by Bandula comes roaring back.

Bandula, suddenly agreeing to my lowballed rate, takes it upon himself to remove my pack, toss it into the back of his tuk-tuk, and before I can speak in my own defense politely *force* me aboard. Taken aback by this brashness, I stop and inform the shyster of his being way too pushy and that as a result I am reluctant to patronize his establishment. To this end Bandula apologizes profusely, reaches out to shake my hand, and begins to employ a brand of cloying conversation that borders on outrageous. Specifically, he points to the skin of his arm and declares it the same as U.S. President Barack Obama's. The comicality inherent in this endeavor, despite it being truly pathetic, does momentarily restore to him a modicum of humility (in my mind), at least enough to edge me back toward accepting the accommodations he offers.

The Thisara Guest House, owned and run by Bandula and family, is located roughly one kilometer south of Old Town Polonnaruwa on a road (more like a hastily paved driveway) deadending at the very *wewa* bund upon which Badulla rampantly works his rounds. It is a grand, two-story multi-colored mansion complete with upper-level balconies, a wraparound yard full of tables and chairs complemented by fountains and hammocks, and a gravel lot of a driveway harboring a dozen stray dogs and cats. Beside the house stands a single-story pink painted cottage — far inferior in size and design — where Bandula and his family reside. Both abodes face a tree line faintly veiling an acre-wide paddy, all set within a low-key residential neighborhood.

After securing my few possesions in my room I accept a complementary ride from Bandula back to the center of town where a man with an upper maxillary projecting outward at at least a forty-five degree angle began talking to me like we were old friends. Turns out he was Bandula's brother (also a tuk-tuk driver) and had recognized me based on description received from Bandual (my scruffy beard and dirty red ball cap probably gave me away).

Upon first impression I find Polonnaruwa unattractive. Decades upon decades of tourists have obviously turned the ruinous jungles here into a veritable resort town catering to the constant wants of westerners (*Free Wi-Fi! Bicycles for Hire! American Breakfast! Tour Guides!*), and it feels far from authentic. Most discouraging though is the costly new Archaeology Museum located behind what was once the Polonnaruwa Rest House. The "museum" serves as the official portal to the ancient city and requires a ticket to enter, the cost of which easily exceeds my own daily food and lodging expenses. However, by deviating off the beaten path I was able to access the ruins of the ancient city without paying the exorbitant ticket price (the ruins of Anuradhapura, after all, are free for one to view). That said, if one does choose to visit the "sacred city" by way of discounting its flimsy perimeter fence, they'd be well advised to exit the same way.

Once among the ruins of medieval Polonnaruwa, however, all other annoyances vanish momentarily as the unassailable merit of Polonnaruwa emerges in all its World Heritage Site glory. The well-preserved ruins of the ancient capital are truly one of the more awesome spectacles to behold on the island and can hold their own (I remain convinced) among the lasting ruins of the world. These include towering brick stupas merely eroded by time, multi-tiered *pokunas* once used for communal bathing, an ornate royal chamber with a boulderous throne resembling a gargoylish lion, monolithic statues carved directly into the towering rock faces — some of the tallest in the word — slabs of smooth stone etched in olden Sanskrit-Sinhala describing the city's founding, and a multitude of other religious and political structures, all of which possess astounding geometric exactitude and celestial-related significance. The architectural marvel of the ancient city, however, is its brick Vatadage, a circular Buddhist temple constructed in the 12th Century during the reign of King Parakrama that during the city's height provided refuge for the sacred tooth relic (the word vatadage literally means "circular relic house").

I remove my shoes and hat (as Buddhist law stipulates) and ascend a number of searing hot steps to enter the Vatadage's round inner chamber (no sort of roofing remains on the structure, if ever it did). Four Buddhas sit crosslegged in lotus praying position, each facing outward at one of the four cardinal directions, as if guarding a central treasure: the Tooth Relic. The structure remains in remarkable condition despite being the oldest building in the "sacred quadrangle." Yet much of the original plaster has chipped off the interior brick walls and one of the four Buddhas now lacks an upper torso, which imbues the shrine with a haunting antiquity.

I wander away from the Vatadage into the surrounding jungle and seat myself momentarily in shade on a low brick ledge to rest. A troop of monkeys migrates over to me in their own standoffish way, and as I finish a small bottle of water I decide to offer the empty plastic to a very unintimidating primate. The creature approaches, takes up the bottle with its hands, places the cap in its mouth, and — very cleverly — uses its feet to twist the bottle counterclockwise. It succeeds in removing the top entirely but only to find not a drop inside the bottle. The monkey cannot further tilt the bottle and so instead drops it and picks up the loose cap and tries to siphon with its tongue what remains. I watch in wonder tinged with guilt, for Polonnaruwa occupies an extremely arid parcel of earth much of the year, and I realize that these monkeys must find a lot of empty plastic bottles.

Come evening I find myself wander along the southern shore of the Parakrama Samudra where the water is low and receded — brilliant green lakebed prime for cattle grazing. I relish the low-lit pastoral scenery, taking photographs of the landscape and observing the very ground beneath my feet. In doing so, two physical anomalies pertaining to the landscape appear to me: 1), far too much sand appears to be present to have been feasibly transported inland from the coast (at least during ancient times), and 2), an overabundance of mussel and clam shells appear similarly out of place. Both elements suggest the landscape may have had some natural origin as a saline sea, or was perhaps the primordial eastern seaboard. Continuing to explore, I come upon a young man with longish hair who does not speak English well enough to satisfy my geologic query but does manage to convey an entire compound sentence with only three words:

"Come. Boat. Elephant."

Behind him bobs a wooden dory that he hand gestures toward. Beyond that, a small island of trees pops up from the center of the lake.

"There?" I ask.

"No. Jungle," he replies.

"How much?"

"One-thousand."

"Maybe tomorrow."

"Five-hundred."

"Maybe tomorrow."

"You smoke?" he asks pleadingly as I walk away.

As the sun sets radiantly on the water I stand facing west-

ward, watching a crowd of Buddhist pilgrims bathe in the tiny wind-rippling waves, their telltale orange robes strewn vividly across the foreground shore. The waning light is perfect, the colors vivid, and the visual ensemble calls to mind a large-scale Andreas Gurskey photograph, every subtle, varying detail perfectly unscripted and profound in its descriptive ability, yet captured within an otherwise everyday scene.

Polonnaruwa ⇨ Batticaloa

1030- The ice-cream man pushes his bicycle through the middle of the Polonnaruwa train yard honking a little toy horn. He peddles frozen treats from an insulated "cool box" strapped to the back.

It's a scorching hot day already as I sit aboard a fully packed train destined for Batticaloa, the end of the line; and in a bit of a tropical paradox I continue to be plagued by a festering cold (snotty nose, slightly sore throat) — nothing too bad but no doubt incurred from my immunities being hampered by something I consumed in Trincomalee. That was five days ago, yet seems like more.

Following a ten minute delay the train takes off, catching back up to the ice-cream man as he too exits the yard, horn still honking. We speed through the outskirts of Kaduruwela, rounding sharp curves you cannot see far ahead of. I read a news brief in the *Daily Mirror* a week back concerning a train traveling this very line to Batticaloa that during the night haphazardly struck two elephants, killing one and sending the other fleeing injured into the brush. This is the reality of where I now am. Most of the island's estimated 1,500 wild elephants live somewhere in the sparsely developed north and in the dense southeastern jungles, the mean geographic center of which I am now passing through. Elephant Crossing signs — identical in design to Deer Crossing signs — now regularly appear along the right of way. So far, the article reported, there have been only two elephant deaths by train this year in Sri Lanka, but that is still more elephant deaths by train than most places in the world!

Beyond the orbital influence of Polonnaruwa, a series of low, pillared viaducts carry the tracks across a parched peneplain. Unforeseeably, this precedes a lengthy bridge spanning the vast Mahaweli Ganga as it flows healthily north toward Trincomalee Bay. Once across the Mahaweli the landscape devolves, turning more and more water-deprived and desolate with each passing mile. In correlating harmony, humanity displays an unmatched tenacity to exist here. Homes constructed by means of sticks, mud, clay, fronds, coir, planks, tarpaulins, and cloth lay claim to the earth, some framed with sticks, others built around the sturdiness of a single tree. It is hard to tell which homes are inhabited and which are not. At one point, as the train sways past an abandoned station, I spot an gigantic pachyderm skull staring back at me from the end of the empty station platform. I have the sudden impulse to leap off the train and retrieve it as some sort of souvenir (were that even logical), but before I can even really consider the option the train has moved on.

Nineteen miles from Batticaloa one of the longer bridges on the island funnels the train across the littoral mouth of the Valaichchenai Lagoon alongside the more modern Batticaloa-Thirukkondaiadimadu-Trincomalee (BTT) Hwy. The sandy white peninsula making up the other side feels increasingly otherworldly. I can feel the moisture in the air and literally taste the salt in it. Tamil/Sinhala graffiti appears increasingly along trackside fences and cinderblock walls, and before I know it we are rolling into battered little Batticaloa.

Batticaloa

I'm just saying, I'm not proud I'm staying at a resort. Be*cause* — yes, the rest house was t*err*ibly overpriced. I mean it must be like the Lonely Planet star recommendation 'cause it was just full of generic tourists. *Ya*, I actually went there. Well I thought it'd be like a normal low-quality place, like in Chilaw. But no, the price was like thrice what I'm paying here. 'Cause, who wants to be traveling alone and staying at res*or*ts? That's like the *loneliest* thing I can think of. I mean it's nice, comparatively. A resort, ya know? It's got a bed with not only a sheet but a blanket too. Usually just my sleeping bag. And the room here's *clean*. Not far really, just like two kilometers. I asked a guy sitting in a tuk-tuk in town. He was young — well I *didn't* know. I guess he just took me to where he had a friend or knew somebody. But ya, the price was more than right so — I was surprised. I mean you should just *see* this little room I'm in — and that's the other thing, here they *have* single rooms, unlike at the rest house. I asked. The room's like a fire lookout. It sits atop this two-story wooden structure like you'd find in the forest. The bottom's like a tool shed or something. Ya, like groundskeeping stuff. I mean there's like stone tables and hammocks and — it's *right* on this lagoon. I mean right on. Ya, a nicer one. Almost like a river. A kilometer or two east. I walked there this afternoon. It's nice. Not built up. Catamaran territory still. A couple cows. Temporary thatch huts that fishermen use for storage and shade. But the current's bad. Ya, like super strong. Not like *big* or anything. It's just like extremely apparent that there's this powerful tidal force that has been *rak*ing these waters northwestwardly for eons and eons and as soon as you step in it just *pulls* you. Ya, but no. I mean I knew better than to fuck with it too much. Plus there's like — I mean in the lagoon back in town you can see just this infes*ta*tion of white jellyfish — like ghost white, *thou*sands — and I was precautious about it, you know, 'cause you figure that since they do come from the sea and all that they'll be concentrated around the shore too. But no. Maybe the current's too strong. Ya, but mostly locals. Only like two others. A couple. I'm staying in a village. Kallady. Ya, like nestled back in a neighborhood. They all are. You know, like dirt roads, no major buildings or commercial centers, lots of large families in small homes. Just like a big crowded residential neighborhood. Not really impoverished, it seems. Ya, the main strip's a *little* built up, coming out of Batticoloa it is but... No, not much. A wine shop, which is nice; a couple of little hotels and groceries. Ya, the bakery kind. Sort of like that but not as dense. Bat*ti*coloa is. I mean I was surprised at its urbanity to tell the truth. It's not junky and dirty like Trincomalee either. No, nicer. Newer somehow. Plus, coming in on the train you really sense the remoteness of this place, compared to the rest of the island I mean. On this low narrow strip of land only good for palm trees to grow that I thought would be like another Kalpitiya experience where there won't even be electricity or a way out other than from which I arrived, but no, Batticaloa's like *bust*ling. Weird change from the deadness of Polonnaruwa, too. Ya, like *sooo* many tourists, but NO ONE stays in town. They're all at high-priced re*sorts* outside of town. Ya, it depends so heavily on tourism and is just fervent with competition between drivers and self-imposed guides. Some people are just too polite to turn them down I guess. It's a small town so it just feels like you're always being followed or something. I couldn't stand it. Two nights. It's nicer here. More anonymity. More open feeling. More public space too. Along the lagoon, which is more like a wide river the town straddles. Benches, parks, stuff out of the ordinary. Ya, but severely infested with milk-white jellyfish — *thou*sands of them. Floating. Propelling themselves around. Whatever milky white jellyfish do. I did see two older men standing in the lagoon water yesterday. Bathing I guess. I mean if you want to catch jellyfish you don't have to stand in the water to do it. Getting better. Ya, I found a pharmacy yesterday but the language barrier thing... I said I had a cold and the pharmacist said "Hot." Then she tried to sell me some medicine for my heart. Like antacid stuff. So I went to like a supermarket pharmacy and asked a kid there 'cause no one else was behind the counter, and he under*stood* me and all and looked for some tablets but I guess they were out 'cause after a minute of looking he said "Finished," and that was all. That's what they say when sold out of something. I've just been like trying to gorge on Vitamin C, which is weird 'cause it's hard to find *juice* juice over here unless it's like a Minute Maid type carbonated juice. Juice here is called nectar, and it's more like juice *con*centrate. Ya, I think I kinda of made myself sick. A little too much mango nectar. The ocean is like ten-minute walk at most. Ya, and what's cool is seeing some of the leftover tsunami destruction. *Seri*-ous. I found this psychedelic Hindu temple today with like the back half, the pyramiding part with all the crazy detailed statuettes, like broken off from the rest of the building and Pisa Tower style all leaning, sunken into the sand. You know, blue-skinned

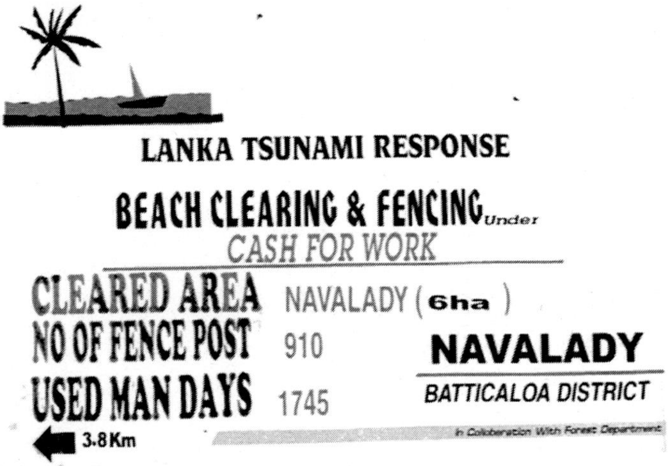

four-armed Vishnus levitating in half-yoga positions, pink elephant gods, deities holding swords, cherubs with angel wings, multi-headed guardians, idolatrous cattle, half-human half-elephant figurines. Ya, looks like a sinkhole just opened up; then you realize the sand has been sucked away, but by something *power*ful. You can just *tell*. Come to think of it, that's probably why this village is so *nice*. I mean most of the homes here are like almost affluent looking. *New*. Colorful. Probably none of what's here now was here ten years ago. I don't know though, I'm just saying: it was probably drastically different. Economically too. People got a chance to rebuild, I guess. The government. Foreign aid. Wouldn't you? And with tourism returning – Batticaloa's not all crumbling like Trincomalee. Maybe not as affected by the war. Only one couple yesterday. But today there's like five more couples. It *does*. I mean doesn't anyone else travel alone? It's like people don't ever do things alone unless they get paid to. Are people just afraid to be alone? That's what I'm *sa*ying though. Like traveling, journeying, whatever, the experience still *matters* if you're the only one that experiences it. But isn't it up to *you* to realize that? Doesn't an experience mean *more* to you if you're the only one experiencing it? Well, that's unfortunate. Because, it's unfortunate people aren't able to appreciate things outside the context of some ro-

mantic or familial relationship. Sure, we all do in different ways. I mean I no more want to push my way of experiencing life on someone than I want theirs forced upon me... I photograph things, for one. To preserve the moment. So it's not lost, or doesn't go forgotten. Well, I feel like I'm accomplishing something just by documenting my experience, especially places I've never been. So I can look back at my life and feel satisfied, like my time was well spent, and have no regrets or wish I did more of something when I had the chance. Then it feels like I've wasted my time, or that an opportunity has been lost. Because what kind of life is it to have no tangible connection to your past? That's almost as bad as not remembering your past. Ya, that's at the core of us all, I think. Self-actualization, like Maslow said. No, as long as it matters to *me*. That's what I'm trying to *say*: we all experience things in different ways, and that's *fine*, I just think it's unfortunate when people are too frightened to experience things on their own. Well, it's like short-changing to others — that kind of existence — especially when one is young and able to experience things on their own. No. There's a difference between being alone and being lonely. Afraid of experiencing boredom, for one, and face uncertainty. Fear of missing out. Boredom, though, can be enlightening, if embraced. I mean like truly considered. A catalyst, in fact. For creativity, and change. Ya, it's their choice, personally I just hate to have to be around it. It's uninspiring to start with. Maybe that's why I like being around Sri Lankans so much — did I tell you that? Once I got over my initial self-consciousness of feeling so out of place here. Sri Lankans don't seek these fulsome lives hinged on social networking, and I can relate to that. They're more in tune with their immediate environment, be it harsh or deprived. The world just feels more insulated here, at least to me it does, like what's beyond the island's borders doesn't matter, and I kind of like that. It's comforting, in a way. Well I notice these things more when traveling alone. Ya, of *course*. I mean it sh*ould*n't be easy. Which reminds me... You know that book I picked up that I told you I was excited about, written by the gal who was returning to India to explore it by train? Big disappointment. I slammed the thing shut with fervor at page 62 when she wrote that after a week of no fastfood a McChicken sandwich was "heaven in a sesame bun." She was traveling with her boyfriend too, who wasn't technically her boyfriend but blah blah blah blah blah. She could have at least lied, like Steinbeck. Ya, adds a new dimension to the experience for sure, but if you're a writer you still need to utilize that aspect in a way that doesn't just detract from the narrative. I mean, I wouldn't be able to write anything of interest here if constantly preoccupied with another. I doubt it. I mean, I inflict too much discomfort on myself in the first place. I walk too much, for one. Probably like ten or twelve kilometers a day — or *miles* I mean. Mostly just exploring. Let's see... I walked to Batticaloa, to like the center of town, then back — that was this morning — then to the ocean and back, which is like a kilometer each way, and but on the way back went out of the way two or three kilometers south, to the next town over. And it was almost unbearably hot out so from there I caught a tuk-tuk back 'cause my thighs were seriously chafing. Little taxi thing. Like one-fifty. No, that's cheap. Honestly though, I think the chafing was mostly due to the sand and salt-water. Ya, real strong. Watery grave is like a common headline in newspapers here. I thought so too at first until I saw it used over and over. Ya, different newspapers. They call it sea-bathing. I guess they do. I know they wash themselves and their clothes in rivers and reservoirs. Not exactly. No, come to think of it up in Trinco where I stayed — that bay I told you about where the water was real placid — I saw a guy bathing in the water there. Didn't think much about it though. Tides of time. Good filtration system.

Batticaloa ⇨ Arugam Bay

Bus slowly moving through town, steadily filling with passengers. The mid-day stifling heat, amplified by the bus's metallic interior, combines with the breeze generated and the shockabsorberless rattle and deep vibrating lull of the motor to render these machines inoculating to me; and with entrancing Indian music pulsating through front-end speakers, and vendors parading down the aisle shouting their wares overtop the electricity of noise, the ride feels intensely surreal. (Outside: bold-colored statues divide the road hooonnk! urban plantain trees dangle golden fruit **BEEEEP! BEEEEP!** green-and-white striped mosque, half-peeled-off election posters **B-B-B-B-BEEP-BEEEEEP!** corrugate-metal homes **HONK** bus-stop children in school-clothes, small family hutches, psychedelic Hindu temple **HONK HONK** rows of catch-all shops selling imported goods, gold-steepled mosque, cattle-driven bullock cart in the middle of the street **HONKKKKK** road snaking south — Mathmunia — **BEEPBEEEEP** moss-covered bricks, "A/C and non-A/C rooms" **BEEEEEEP** teal-painted concrete facades, plantain fronds the size of elephant ears, cheap plastic toy shops and cell-phone accessory shops HORN! HORN! HORN! HORN! HORN! "Sharma," motorbike blowing through a crosswalk HONK Esuaren Hotel, Airtel, Sampath Bank, log trucks **HHHHHHHHHHOOONK** Tasty Mutty Shop "No EGB No Food!" HONK City Hotel, Methodist Hali **honk** Siyenko Traders, shoe-repairman on sidewalk beneath umbrella shade **BBZZTTBBZZTT** tuk tuk tuk tuk tuk tuk tuktuktuktuktuktuktuktuktuk Shenuja Tailors, Choice Place, Gold House **HONK!** Empty dirt lot serving as makeshift side-of-the-road bus depot, murder on a balcony *ka-ka. ka-ka* wood-and-metal scrap-built huts, "Vidyala" HONK Dialog Lanka, Moleen Hotel **HONK!** grand mosque with a crumbling façade, "Majeedia" honk ornamental archways peeling paint **BEEEEEEP! BEEP!** Nippor Cement, fresh-caught fish market, king coconuts "For Sale" honk Stalinesque Rajapaksa posters the size of billboards h-h-h-h-honk-honnnnk! untethered cattle and hay tractor clogging street **HONK** intricately designed Hindu temple complex **HONK** Saudia Tyre House, Haj Traval **BEEP BEEEEEEP BEEP** Razeek Trade Centre, freshly plowed farm plots **BZZZT** and irrigated fields and muddy tracts huuuunnnnngggggk distant knobs rising pronouncedly on the western horizon, teal stuccos **HONK** olive-green mosque **HONK** — km 371, Hwy A4 — cloudy to the west **HONK!** man pedaling bicycle with basket on front handlebars past white and pine-green striped mosque, Aliza Cool Spot HORN! **BEEP-BEEEEEEP!** Sujath Cycle Works, large hemp-looking plants **BZZZT-BZZZZT** young girls walking beneath shade of polkadot umbrella, women wearing black veils **HONK** "Atlas: Be Creative," Hotel Foreign Food & Bakery **HONK** Fashion Steel Works, lumbering cement truck *BBBRRRRNNNNNKKKK* marshy lagoons east, men shirtless and saronged and shoeless fixing tractor **HONK** "You Plant A Tree," Lavanna Food City, white and pine-green striped mosque bEEEEEp-bEEEp! Jamaldeen Traders, Lanka Stores, Shawmugga Gift Place **HOOOONNNNKKK!** . . .)

Before I know it the bus has arrived in Kalmunai, a buzzing little coastal road of a town twenty-five miles south of Batticaloa where I am told to deboard. Kalmunai is the end of the line for this bus, and what becomes immediately clear is that any traveler south of Batticaloa is assumed to be en route to Arugam Bay. This is a local no-brainer. Even if you're *not* headed to Arugam Bay, say because you've never *heard* of Arugam Bay, you will soon know of Arugam Bay and likely end up there because it is the main tourist destination on the island's entire east coast and so every local assumes it is *your* target destination, too (and honestly, these little towns along the way probably don't care for the influx of tourists and would just as soon pass them off to Arugam Bay in order to preserve their own way of life a little while longer).

Not to be disappointed, both the bus driver and fare collector automatically instruct me to wait across the street for a connecting bus to Arugam Bay. I do as advised but don't really know where to stand and so end up waiting in front of some nominal shoe bodega like a goon. Within seconds a tuk-tuk driver offers me a ride straight to Arugam Bay, and before I can answer tells me to come with him that he will take me there in his tuk-tuk no problem. I can only imagine how many he's enticed before, travelers fed up with overcrowded suicidal bus rides, feeling like high society simply because they can afford a five- or six-thousand rupee fare. Not me; nor do I have those kinds of rupees to spare.

After a minute or two another man, a hotel owner, seeing me looking bewildered, rescues me by ushering me through his restaurant and out the back door — one street over — to where another group of buses stand in a dusty red lot beneath the merciless sun. The man points to a specific hulking red means of transportation with chipped yellow Sinhala signage painted on its side (and that looks like all the other buses) and tells me *that's* the bus to Arugam Bay. I thank him by purchasing a bottle of water from his shop, and then quickly cross the street to board. But not so fast; the bus is completely full. And not wishing to stand midaisle on the overcrowded machine for the next two hours, I opt to be patient and wait for the next bus. But like I said, people just *assume* you're going to Arugam Bay, and as soon as the fare collector spots me he jumps off, grabs my pack, throws it behind the driver's seat (the only space to store oversized baggage on the bus), and urges me aboard as the bus begins to roll and leaving me no choice but to hop on.

Come Akkaraipattu, fifteen *more* raucous miles south, the bus again empties. I thought I was in for a straight shot to Arugam Bay but that is not the case. Of course the bus driver knows where I am headed and so directs me appropriately across the lot to another like bus, its destination Pottuvil, located twenty-nine miles *further* south, across from which lies the idyllic bay of Arugam.

I board the new bus to an empty window seat and wait in the glaring sun for the next twenty minutes as the machine fills and fills and fills to an unbe*lie*vable capacity. More stand than sit. I feel bad for the old men and women, and the children, who have to ride standing, gasping for air, vulnerable and helpless in case of a sudden jolt or — just as likely — some collision. But no one else sacrifices their seat so I do not feel compelled to either. Besides, my displacement would only cause such a disturbance within the already-cram-packed bus as to be deemed counterproductive. Not to mention the guy standing closest me in the aisle would likely be the one to subsume the seat since no one seems to view senior citizens as more deserving (although some buses do occasionally have signs posted in the front to reserve seats for pregnant women but that mostly goes unheeded and is probably left over from the days of Ceylon). Regardless, no means of transportation, particularly one that serves the public, should be permitted to operate under such a burden of overwhelming capacity as this. Not only does the overflow of passengers pose hazard to the driver's visibility and maneuverability, and not only must it hamper the fare collector's ability to perform *his* job safely, but as a passenger I cringe at the lack of oversite and the deliberate disregard of any sort of — people not only crowd the aisle of the bus but stand exposed to traffic on the footboards of both the front and rear exits), yet off we go, thundering down a narrow two-lane highway laid across the sandy, low-lying earth.

Before I know it, after nodding off into a gentle sloom amid the craze of the roadway, we arrive in Pottuvil, a cramped coastal municipality located on a wildlife-infused lagoon directly across from Arugam Bay. No one goes to Pottuvil unless they're going to Arugam Bay — everyone knows this — and before my feet ever touch the ground, before the bus even *stops*, a hefty tuk-tuk driver singles me out aggressively, shouting indiscernibly at me in Sinhala while also repeating "Arugam Bay. Arugam Bay." What a way to wake: dazed, covered in sweat, a robust man targeting me through a halfway-open window before I even know where I am.

Alas, I am the only Caucasian person on the bus, and the hefty driver is there to subsume me upon stepping off, his actions in full compliance with what seems the common law of the land, that the first (and in most cases most aggressive) driver gets the tourist. Everyone else stands back like it is my fate to be fed to the man, and after five hours of cramped sweltering bus rides, compounded with the resignation I suddenly feel at being so easily compromised, I acquiesce.

By now I am well aware that many tuk-tuk drivers work for or are at least affiliated with certain guest houses and resort-hotels, and that those places reward drivers who bring them clients, and so of course I first get pummeled with *Do* I need a room and *Where* exactly am I staying, etc, etc. And again, exhausted from the already taxing journey, and wary of the fact that I will only have to put up with a dozen more relentless solicitors once I arrive in Arugam Bay since I *don't* yet have a place to stay, I give in. I figure, *Why not?* The man's not going to force me anywhere I don't want to go (other than out of Pottuvil), and I am comfortable enough now to simply not agree to pay some outrageous rate or fare (I usually ask beforehand anyway). Besides, if Arugam Bay is as paradisiacal as I have heard, then one place will be just as good as the next.

*

1430- At the northern end of Arugam Bay, just across the lagoon, the tuk-tuk driver turns left onto a sandy beachside alley appropriately denoted Beach Hut Road. Various lodgings describe each side, along with — surprise! — numerous beach huts. The first such lodging we come to happens to be entirely full, a man lounging on an outdoor couch says without bothering to stand. We then move on to the neighboring place, a laid-back surfer lodge where on a shaded patio a shirtless blonde guy with a primal shoulder tattoo lies recumbent on a picnic table bench, passed out or sleeping. Around him sit other beach bums, eating, drinking, and laughing like at summer camp while young Sri Lankan staffers mill about inefficiently like stoners (picking things up, sitting things back down, attending to the stereo while nodding in rhythm to the music, serving food, adding a chuckle when appropriate). I get the immediate sense that nothing here matters outside the surf and sun and the appearance of one's own body, and that at first horrifies me. The last thing I want is to be around a bunch of wave-catching tourists in some over-priced hostel. But then again I knew that in coming here I would at least have to put up with some of this, so again I just go with it.

The tuk-tuk driver is obviously known here and acknowledged right away by a skinny, scruffy Sri Lankan kid who, upon looking up from some unbustled task, gives a calm thumbs up. He then ambles over, thanks the driver, and leads me back a sandy pathway into a shaded compound where a dozen or so thatched-roof shelters can be found. Only two spaces are available: a small treehouse *cabana* near the entrance that I admit looks alluring for 1,200 rupees (pretty cheap), and a large, dimly lit garage-like room in the rear for 600 rupees (even cheaper!). I choose the less-than-cozy but more practical 600-rupee hut (cold-water shower out back, which doubles as urinary restroom) since I have no one to impress, and head for the beach.

Arugam Bay

Truth: Arugam Bay comprises a little crumb of heaven carved into the superlative southeast Sri Lankan seashore. The town is small enough that development is limited but vibrant enough to attract and retain a constant array of travelers, especially during the dry season when endless sunshine and sea breeze pay compliment to its cool aqua-tinted water and golden sand.

Fact: Arugam Bay functions as a popular tourist destination despite being largely cut off from the rest of the island by rugged mountains and an aggregate of national parks, wildlife sanctuaries, and forest reserves where roads don't penetrate (access remains confined to a single two-lane highway coming down from the north while all roads south ultimately lead nowhere and/or impassible for much the year due to flooding and natural erosion). This does not deter determined travelers who go to great lengths and often endure personal discomfort to reach Arugam Bay year-round. As a result, the town tends to retain visitors once they have arrived, making it a kind of End of The Road location for many.

Fact: The quickest way to reach Arugam Bay is to fly from Colombo aboard a little jet (here called an "air taxi") to the dinky Ampara airport — an hour-long flight at most — and from there submit to a one- to two-hour bus or tuk-tuk ride southeast to the coast. However, the expensiveness of that option appeals to only the privileged few. For the rest of us our travel options are thus:

> **A)** take an overnight (Eastern Line) train clear across the island to Batticaloa where come morning one must access three consecutive buses south — first to Kalmunai, then Akkaraipattu, and finally Pottuvil, which is just across the lagoon from Arugam Bay — all in all a fifteen- to twenty-hour trek (this is how I arrived);
>
> **B)** ride inland from Colombo on the Upcountry Line to Badulla (an eight to ten hour run to begin with), then take a bus down from the mountains to Monara-

gala and another to Pottuvil — a fifteen to twenty-hour trek total; or **C)** ride the Coast Line three-and-a-half hours south to Matara, take a bus east to Hambantota, then a succession buses north and northeast, first to Wellaweya, then to Monaragala, and finally to Pottuvil — another all-day affair!

Alternative Option: Of course one could just skip all the ten-hour train rides and self-sabotaging bus crap and hire a personal driver to take you straight to Arugam Bay from Colombo, but that would be spendy, and good luck finding someone to drive you such distance on short notice. Besides, a straight-shot ride would likely take just as long because the roads of Sri Lanka do not discriminate.

Truth: There may be little is there to do in Arugam Bay aside from gourmandizing (selectively), fornicating (if you have the opportunity), and indulging in the sea, sand, and sun (unabashedly), but that does not detract in the least from the pure sublimity of the locale. While surfing, sunning, and swimming are the mainstay, one can also windsurf (if they have the means), charter a tuk-tuk to take them around the area on a sort of impromptu wildlife safari, or even try their hand at some primitive methods of fishing, as learned from the locals.

Personal Itinerary: My days in Arugam Bay start with casually waking, walking a few steps from my room to the beach, strolling the sand south in search of some breakfast but more importantly a pot of coffee (one that's *not* sludge), hunting down an English language newspaper around 9 A.M. when newspapers arrive from wherever they're printed, returning to the beach to peruse said newspaper in the morning's finest rays (three newspapers if it's Sunday), perhaps sipping some tea instead of sludgy coffee since I am in a country where some of the world's very finest tea is grown, intermittently wading into the sea to cool off and stretch and urinate — basically living the life of beach bum — till around 11 when the local hotels put out rice and dhal curry and paratha or roti for lunch, eating cheaply at some local hotel (often working up a sweat due to Sri Lankan food being inherently spicy), returning to the beach to rinse off in the water (potentially locating an area mid-bay where the waves mount the largest and, by figuring out a sort of inconsistent tidal pattern, catching a pronounced surge rather far out and bodysurfing the wave in), until starting to feel a little childish and so instead setting off to explore the beach directly south of the bay where sand-dunes three- and four-stories high offer a sweeping view of the entire bay as well as the vast ocean east where much stronger winds reign and more affluent visitors harness those winds to sail and windsurf, eventually returning to the beach and perhaps purchasing a king coconut from a local beachside proprietor for no more than 50 rupees and, after the proprietor hacks a triangulated hole in the top and inserts a non-degradable plastic straw for drinking, drinking the exfoliating water contained therein and handing the empty fruit back so that the man can scrape out the meat for himself to have (if he so desires), finding some nearby shade to lie in in order to read one of several books (including *One Hundred Years of Solitude*, by Gabriel Garcia Marquez, a title I feel I can currently relate to), or write, invariably imbibing a cold Lion Lager to help corral focus before eventually returning to the surfer squat to rinse the accrued salt and sand off my body in the solar shower and/or take a brief nap to recharge myself in order to ultimately return to the beach post-sundown and select a restaurant to dine at, some fancied-up-for-night beachside hotel with a table in the sand, the tide lapping at its legs and a cool breeze wobbling a candle's flame under the auspices of a moon high and bright.

Fact: Arugam Bay is known as one of the top surfing locales in this part of the world. The natural contours of the bay corral incoming ocean currents into long, low waves ideal for sport and every year contests are held in Arugam Bay, attracting amateur surfers from all over the globe, especially Australia, to whom Sri Lanka serves as a favorite respite during the antipodean winter.

Falsehood: Arugam Bay is today too overdeveloped and crowded for one to relax and really enjoy.

Truth: When the Boxing Day tsunami struck the island in 2004 the wave first impacted the island's southeast coast, and with force unmatched. Lagoons were disgorged, trees uprooted, homes unmoored, farms destroyed, and then the wave retracted like a whirlpool, dragging all it had upended back to sea, including scores of swollen bodies. For a number of weeks afterward Arugam Bay, along with all locales to the south, remained accessible only by boat or air, further deepening the crevice of destruction wrought while prolonging the period of recovery. A decade later coastal plots still stand denuded and the greater area remains largely underdeveloped. No familiar eateries or chain restaurants prosper here like in Colombo and elsewhere, and the majority of lodgings still resemble bungalows and thatch-roof huts. And although there do exist several large and fancy-looking resorts, these also look like they have been open barely a week. In fact, the coastline remains surrounded by such dense jungle growth that upon arriving here via tuk-tuk my driver pointed casually across the Arugam Lagoon to a wild elephant knee deep in the gob, visible from the common roadway.

Fact: Arugam Bay is at its core a bustling fishing village called Ulla, which an old metallic roadside sign still stands to proclaim, and where Ulla is most concentrated — commanding prime beachfront real estate mid-bay amidst a clutter of colorful catamarans, tangled trawls, and flimsy metal storage sheds — also happens to stand the newest, largest, fanciest resort in Arugam Bay: The Bay Vista Hotel. Needless to say, The Bay Vista Hotel does not appear to be "hopping" in any sense of the word and beach access remains hindered by Ulla's unkempt seafood storage area and as-far-from-hipster-as-one-can-imagine generational fishermen who every dawn set out upon the somber morning sea to cast trawls to the depths of the ocean floor, returning with their day's catch before most have awakened. The Bay Vista Hotel, while lavish looking on the exterior, appears constantly devoid of activity, its occupants clearly having wandered elsewhere to apricate.

> **Resulting Truth:** Arugam Bay very much remains Ulla villager territory; after that it belongs to the crows; then to the dogs. Tourists and travelers, although often outnumbering locals, maintain the presence of a geist — ephemeral and inconsequential to how Arugam Bay ultimately functions and what it retains.

Initial Impression: Arugam Bay feels like a hybrid Sri Lankan Australia. While this may seem more psychological than physical, it's difficult to overlook the prominence of English speaking Caucasian surfers here with strong Australian accents intermingling bro-like with long-haired *Lankan* kids who *also* surf and *also* speak pretty good English and employ all the same surfer euphemisms and lingo and just generally have the same Attitude. It's like somewhere along the way the Australian surfing community adopted tiny Arugam Bay as its home away from home, its little brother.

> **Secondary Impression:** Considering the above, along with beachfront guest houses with names such as "Galaxy Room," "Water Music," and "Stardust," Arugam Bay does feel like its the hippest location on the island. A more over-handed indictor of this cultural status, however, may be the graffiti art present: actual sophisticated, high-technicality spray-painted "pieces." Typically, graffiti correlates with urban size and degree of commercial assimilation. Yet not so in Sri Lanka where Colombo almost totally in lacks street art yet tiny Arugam Bay, one of the more removed vicinities on the island, somehow possesses *more* graffiti within its few-acre radius (albeit probably totally legal). This, to me, is most telling because graffiti has become largely a bourgeois sport — not only is spray paint expensive nowadays but good quality spray paint is extremely hard to come by here; considering the many vibrant hues coloring the walls around Arugam Bay, this paint could only have been brought here from overseas. The work is undoubtedly that of European and Australian artists, but the mere presence of it here illustrates the level of cultural immersion at hand: nowhere else on the island do impoverished building owners permit their landholdings to be muralized by foreign hands.

True story: On my first day in Arugam Bay I stopped a very serious looking man who was carrying a newspaper to inquire as to where I might obtain one of my own. Upon conversation further initiated by him we got to talking about the whole *What is your country* thing and he told me that he teaches English at a school in Arugam Bay and that he was once supposed to travel to America to appear on *Good Morning America*, the reason being that after the Tsunami he rescued a baby and the baby was sent to *Good Morning America* — or something along those lines — but then somethingoran-other happened to obstruct his going to America and that was very disappointing to him. He said that an author from Canada later arrived and spent 70 days in Arugam Bay doing recovery work and writing about him and the Tsunami, that he could show me the resultant book — it was in his classroom. That book is titled: *Tsunami Journey, Seventy Days in Sri Lanka.*

Truth (although not pertaining specifically to Arugam Bay): At eateries in Sri Lanka one never can predict the quality of food served, and while this total lack of predictability can be refreshing, it does invariably lead to some disappointing meals, along with the more delightful ones.

Example (pertaining to Arugam Bay): At the Perhera Restaurant in Arugam Bay, a meek, family-run, house-converted diner, the service proved amiable and prompt but the meal arrived cold — cold rice, cold dhal, and lukewarm greens. However, at Rika's, an automotive-repair-shop-looking hotel that I would hardly've noticed this afternoon had it not been for the nexus of flies amassed out front (which I had difficulty avoiding), the service proved slow and uncertain to the point that I wondered if the place was actually open right up until my meal arrived, and but my *god* the food was fantastic — fresh, tasteful, plentiful, and best of all searing *hot*. Prices were about the same at both but judging by appearance you would never have known the true discrepancy.

Fact: Beer in Arugam Bay, especially Lion Lager, can be acquired at just about any restaurant or hostel, and with no IDing nonsense; yet beer in Arugam Bay also happens to be the most expensive beer on the island, and that's not taking into account the rs. 40 bottle deposit automatically tacked on by retailers (which is kind of a lot considering 40 rupees in Sri Lanka amounts to pretty standard bus fare). The real kicker though is that restaurants and hostels in Arugam Bay also, very cleverly, militantly repossess empty bottles in order to redeem for them*selves* the hefty bottle deposit already fronted by *you*. At the low-cost surfer squat where I am currently staying, for example, a 22 oz. of Lion runs rs. 300, more than *twice* as much as one normally costs (and half the cost of my room)!

True Story (pertaining to the above): Thinking that I might venture outside town and find cheaper libations, or perhaps a stronger elixir, like Old Keg whiskey (note: whiskey is *not* sold at the central Arugam Bay beer store — only beer), I flagged down a tuk-tuk with a driver who understood what I was after and informed me I could obtain whiskey at Food City in Pottuvil (a grocery chain that oftentimes does have small in-store liquor stores), and that he'd give me a lift there and back for only rs. 400 no problem, which, even if steep, was in line with what I paid to get *to* Arugam Bay from Pottuvil in the first place (which was rs. 200). So off we went at sunset, the large orange disc descending picturesquely onto the murky Arugam Lagoon against a gentle mauve sky. Once we arrived in Pottuvil, however, the folks at Food City only shrugged at the misinformation I'd received because Pottuvil, it turns out, happens to be a dry town, as in alcohol intolerant. What then immediately became apparent was that the tuk-tuk driver — a polite enough fellow — did not know what he was talking about and probably didn't even drink alcohol for the sake of his religion. Upon exiting the store empty handed a second driver then became involved (although by that time I was more frustrated about being duped into accepting a taxi ride to an alcohol intolerant town and that I was now going to get joyridden *back* and no matter what would have to pay the fare). The second driver, however, did inform the first that at the far end of Arugam Bay lurked a dubious local bar that purportedly also *sold* bottles of liquor. And so off we went back across the Arugam Lagoon, the carmine orb now almost entirely submerged on the rippling surface water. The tuk-tuk continued past the Arugam Bay beer store toward the south end of town, obeyed the sharp inward curving road just past Ulla, then immediately veered right onto a tamped dirt and gravel affair, and followed that back into the jungle, and just when I thought we were going to end up in the lagoon with the sun a shady dive bar emerged and the tuk-tuk came to a skidding to a halt. There, situated on the southern shore of the Arugam Lagoon (or some sub-lagoon), stood a drink-in liquor store crowded like at happy hour with all variety of Ulla fishermen. Behind the counter, sandwiched between bottles of scotch and arrack, sat the only whiskey they carried: Old Keg. At the request of my tuk-tuk driver the bartender retrieved a pint for me, and although I wasn't too thrilled on the price of it, I figured it'd end up saving some rupees in the long-run. Plus, after the whole tuk-tuk ordeal I felt I needed to make it worth my while and come away with something. The transaction thus commenced rapidly, the tuk-tuk driver monitoring me from behind like I might try to run off without paying the fare, and before I knew it he was escorting back to his tuk-tuk. I was then driven back to the spot I was original picked up at (near the beer store), but before I paid the man what I felt he de*served* for taking me on a five-kilometer joyride (this is business after all) I inquired how much *he* thought I owed him, and, oh... six-hundred rupees he told me. ⊠ We shared a pleasant laugh while he realized I'm not as gullible as some, and I paid the shyster half of what he asked for and told him he was lucky to get even that. Then, upon returning to the surfer squat, where I received a classic thumbs-up from a Sri Lankan kid who upon seeing my bottle of whisky remarked "good medicine," I was told that the going rate to Pottuvil and back is rs. 200 so not to worry, that the guy still got a good rate.

Truth: At 0530 I awoke to someone singing venerably on the patio outside the very door behind which I slept. I figured that A), they must be crazy, or B), fanatically devout, but no doubt, C), were oblivious to my being asleep inside.

Fact: The mosque down the street airs Muslim prayer recordings thrice a day over loudspeakers beginning at five-thirty A.M., a voice withering in song. These broadcasts are loud enough to wake one and clear enough to cause one unfamiliar with their regularity to in a half-asleep haze think the sound originating right outside their door.

Truth: A stereo located in the dining area of the surfer squat where I am staying was this evening playing Detroit Michigan's The White Stripes very loudly, to which numerous Sri Lankans and Australians were leg-tapping and head-bobbing along to subconsciously. (I believe the song was the thrubbing rhythmic "The Hardest Button to Button" off the *Elephant* album.)

Realization: It's remarkable how generically proud one can unexpectedly come to feel when traveling in a foreign country and they hear a familiar song from their home country that is being recognized and enjoyed by individuals of different nationalities, but none who can claim the same creative kinship. Alas, global mainstream artistry is an export power few nations possess equal to that of the United States (certainly not tiny Sri Lanka), but it would be fundamentally false to think that this "mainstream artistry" is not comprised of a broad patchwork of talent extending to almost every corner of the globe. The rapper M.I.A., for example, who was born in London and now lives and works in Los Angeles, is actually an ethnic Tamil who came of age living in Northern Sri Lanka during the civil war. Her real name is Mathangi Arulpragasam, and she became an international sensation after her song "Paper Planes" was featured in the award-winning film *Slumdog Millionaire*, set in India (that and for performing alongside Madonna at the Super Bowl XLVI halftime show and infamously extending her middle-finger politely to the entire televised viewing audience). Her father, Arul Pragasam, was a Tamil resistant fighter, and following in his footsteps she spoken out against the Sri Lankan government concerning human rights.

> (**Fact:** MIA was, in retaliation, sued by the NFL for breach of contract and lack of regard for values to the sum of 1.5 million dollars, to which MIA counter-sued the NFL claiming that the scantily clad, sexually provocative cheerleaders present were certainly more offensive than her mere hand gesture.)

Imperial Observation: The main road through Arugam Bay — Panama Road —

along which everyone must travel to get anywhere, happens to be heavy policed, although mostly after dark I notice. Elsewhere on the island (in Colombo and such), it's the other way around: illicit venders prosper knowingly after dark from *lack* of police presence whilst unregistered tuk-tuks confidently run their rounds. But in Arugam Bay come sundown vigilant lawmen stand watch at the edge of town where the road funnels all vehicles across the lagoon. They use flashlights to signal tuk-tuks to the roadside for minor otherwise unnoticeable infractions or coordinate ahead to waiting officers to do the same. This authoritative presence correlates approximately to the influx of foreign travelers, and so is understandable compared to, say, Pottuvil. However, this is not to suggest that life in Arugam Bay ever denigrates to Spring Break-like out of control. Never. Arugam Bay remains very low-key, and the heavy police presence seems to function not to intimidate so much as maintain law and order. In fact, it may exist primarily to deter competing drivers from overcrowding Arugam Bay and taking advantage of travelers and tourists in nefarious ways, thus preserving the town as a preferred destination for travelers.

> **Fact (relating to the above):** Less than ten years ago both Pottuvil and Arugam Bay were prone to spurts of violence and extremism, caught on the fringe of territory contested by the Tamil Tigers, a dispute at the center of the island's three-decade-long civil war.

Idealistic Instances: With an almost total lack of light pollution the nighttime shoreline in Arugam Bay appears nearly pitch-black; only the moon, backdropped by the low pulse of parsec-distant stars, faintly illuminates the frothing of the sea. With singular flames dancing upon restaurant tables with legs in the sand, and cozy dinners taking place at small eateries tucked back in the darkness off the main road, I am reminded of cool summer nights in some chic Brooklyn, New York neighborhood.

> **Response:** After three idyllic days here surrounded by so many blissful, beautiful human beings who *all* happen to be in the company of a significant other, I have begun to resent this place of my dreams while silently lamenting my own loves lost.

Final Thoughts: The convivial blending of this prosaic fishing village deep-rooted in the age-old tenets of Islam, Buddhism, and Hinduism, with the free-spirited, overprivileged nature of the First World, on a remote stretch of underdeveloped SE Asian coast thrice removed from any major city, makes Arugam Bay one of if not the most austere yet still remarkably socially progressive locations on planet Earth. Nowhere else have I witnessed modern fashions so seamlessly integrated into the lives of everyday islanders, and the care-free attitudes and lifestyles of vacationers so naturally accepted and reciprocated. This juxtaposition at times does appear stark and downright surreal, and in that sense Arugam Bay does conjure some disbelief, such as on my last day in Arugam Bay when a rickety wooden bullock cart with creaky oversized wheels comes rolling down the middle of the main coastal road at 2 kmph, its shirtless saronged old driver whipping the scrawny bovine past a wall painted with European pop-art graffiti, a wall belonging to a modern surf shop called *Shred Shop* where a tall Caucasian blonde and her prime-physiqued boyfriend converse convivially with a local proprietor who speaks their language only scantily yet enthusiastically, an improbable marriage of class, culture, and respective histories further accentuated by a mangy stray scuttling past on three good legs, unwanted but undeterred, toward a breathtaking seascape of timeless attributes.

PART III: ONWARD

Arugam Bay ⇨ Hambantota

1100- One has not experienced the full *thrall* of Sri Lankan travel until they have traveled aboard an absolutely cram-packed city bus and forced to stand, center aisle, for the entirety of a two-hour journey along some lone manic mountain highway. Just when you think the bus can't *possibly* take on another passenger, the driver slams on the brakes and — no need to open the doors because there *are* no doors and half a dozen people ride the footboards — *more* people cram on; just when you think the bus can't possibly manage the uphill passing on the narrow two-lane road it is accelerating to attempt, just when the lorry it is attempting to pass cannot be tailed any closer without being backrammed, just *then* the bus veers into the oncoming lane directly toward a small motorbike carrying a father and mother and in the mother's arms an infant with no cranial protection, RPMs *scream*ing, horn blasting, mercilessly forcing the mother-father-helmetless-infant-carrying motorbike to the loose-gravel shoulder; just when you think the crush of bodies on board cannot further compress for the sake of basic transpiration and circulation, that other riders can't *poss*ibly be expected to endure more physical discomfort without openly revolting, just then a passenger somewhere in the thick of the pack begins to work their way off, their initial movement setting off a chain-reaction that translates to a centrifugal melding of bodies further aided by the bus careening along a curving stretch of road; just when you think your life cannot be any more imperiled, that the bus cannot operate any more blatantly in violation of any and all public safety requirements and regulations, just *then* a patrolman appears ahead signaling the bus to the side of the road, *finally*, you think, to put a compulsory end to this death ride it now becomes apparent must be some outlandish hijacking you've so unluckily found yourself aboard, the bus now swerving toward the uniformed patrolman with vindictive aim in order to slow *just* enough for that officer to step aboard and commence jovial backpatting *tête-à-tête* with the juvenile bus driver in a way that becomes apparent is perfectly routine and all in good jest as the bus continues up the road to the Police Academy where it again slows maliciously and the officer smiles graciously and waves bye as he steps off; just when you think the entire sure-to-be-fatal rolling catastrophe cannot get any more outrageous in its final throes, just when you think you've seen all you could *poss*ibly conjure transportation-wise within the duration of a single town-to-town commute, just *then* a human can be discerned squeezing through the certified mash of bodies clogging the aisle, chanting invisibly overtop the bus's deafening stereo speakers pumping out love ballads sung by popular Sinhalese crooners, the soundtrack accompanied by video beaming from a television screen adhered to the front ceiling above the driver's seat, a pre-recorded concert by a reggae influenced *ramba* group that looks like it is from the 1980s until the singers — all men dressed in stark white groomsmen suits — suddenly jump into an impromptu Singhalese version of "Gangnam Style," just *then* the invisible chanter manifests at your knees, a legless mendicant moving through on some sort of palleted skateboard while rattling a decrepit handful of coins, all happening with such bland routine that everyday seated passengers have gently nodded off to sloom.

Although I have at times found the clanking innocuous drone of Sri Lankan buses subduing, that particular sentiment remains far from mind during this disturbing leg of travel. For two nerve-wracking hours this impromptu moving bazaar traces a cracked ribbon of concrete up the backside of the rugged Uva Province, weaving through boulderous precipices jutting from the earth like enormous black teeth, and after the first hour I have a clear view ahead of the anarchy unleashed upon the road. On two separate occasions the bus barely avoids head-on collisions with grazing cattle, its wheels assaulting the gravel shoulder with such teeth-rattling intensity that an old woman across the aisle from me is nearly thrown from her seat.

Upon arrival in Monaragala I stumble from one death machine but waste no time boarding another, and do so early enough to claim a seat. However, with several minutes to spare before departure (the driver has not yet arrived) nature calls and I chance leaving my bag aboard the idle bus while I cross the littered lot to a public restroom. That ungodly building could not possibly have been mistaken for anything other than what it was. It is attended to by a debilitated man stationed on a cot between the Ladies and Gentlemen's doors intent on collecting from everyone who exits ten rupees for their pity. After contributing to the rancid stench of sewage I too pay the man for I don't know exactly what. Then, looking back across the lot, I see the very bus I recently trusted my bag aboard now departing. I hustle frantically back and just barely succeed in reclaiming my seat, yet the bus is another my nerves would be better off had I never boarded.

Bus operators and fare collectors in Sri Lanka, while by and large a dependable and hard-working lot who *can* be trusted not to rip you off, do not on the other hand perform well in the realm of public safety. Case in point: the driver steering this doomed automobile across the mountains – first to Wellawaya, then south to Hambantota – nearly runs an approaching cement truck off the road while attempting to pass a slow-moving lorry along a section of road well-posted with cautions signs, including those warning of *elephants* crossing! The kid (I swear I can see his molars just beginning to emerge when he stuffs his mouth with wads of betel to chew) drives like all the others, like he is *trying* to kill the clutch. At one point a crowd of aspiring passengers gathered roadside begin to wave frantically as the bus approaches, likely because they do not think the driver sees them. Indeed, the bus continues to accelerate until its front fender reaches the crowd, and only *then* does the driver slam on the brakes with

implied fury and bring the rear skidding to a near-halt mere feet from their faces, never really stopping, taunting those who dare to board to chance it on the fly. And this is not the only time such recklessness is displayed. Repeatedly I bear witness to some poor child on their way home from school attempting to board, stepping toward the bus in shoddy sandals as the driver teases the breaks before speeding back up and causing the child to life-riskingly *leap* onto the rear step as the bus roars off kicking up dust.

And dare not ye attempt to alight! If one wishes off, and even goes so far as to inform the driver as to where, the result is the same: the bus swerves onto the unpaved shoulder near the specified junction and slows just enough for the passenger if they want off all that badly to *jump*. This endures fifty godforsaken miles to Hambantota. The bus streaming, careening, steadily throttling away at nerves.

*

1800- Step off into the frigidity and coldness of the real world. Nothing pretty here. A disfigured statue of some saronged old fisherman (or pirate) stands along the island's south shore before a cluttered harbor, its limbs dangling by wire, shins broken-off exposing rebar skeleton. Something that survived the tsunami. Grown men grab at me, tell me they're my friend, that they've been waiting for my arrival all afternoon. But the truth is, in these littered streets I am no more wanted than fresh scourge of dengue fever.

I wander uphill through a low-income residential neighborhood in the waning hour of light, an immense sand dune buffering homes from the surging sea. Children chase after me, stipulating that I give them rupees for using a camera on them I did not use. They harass, harangue and heckle me down a never-ending street; and a group of cricket-bat wielding fifteen-year-olds repeatedly threaten my life.

Where else in Sri Lanka but Hambantota do children know only enough English to say they'll kill you?

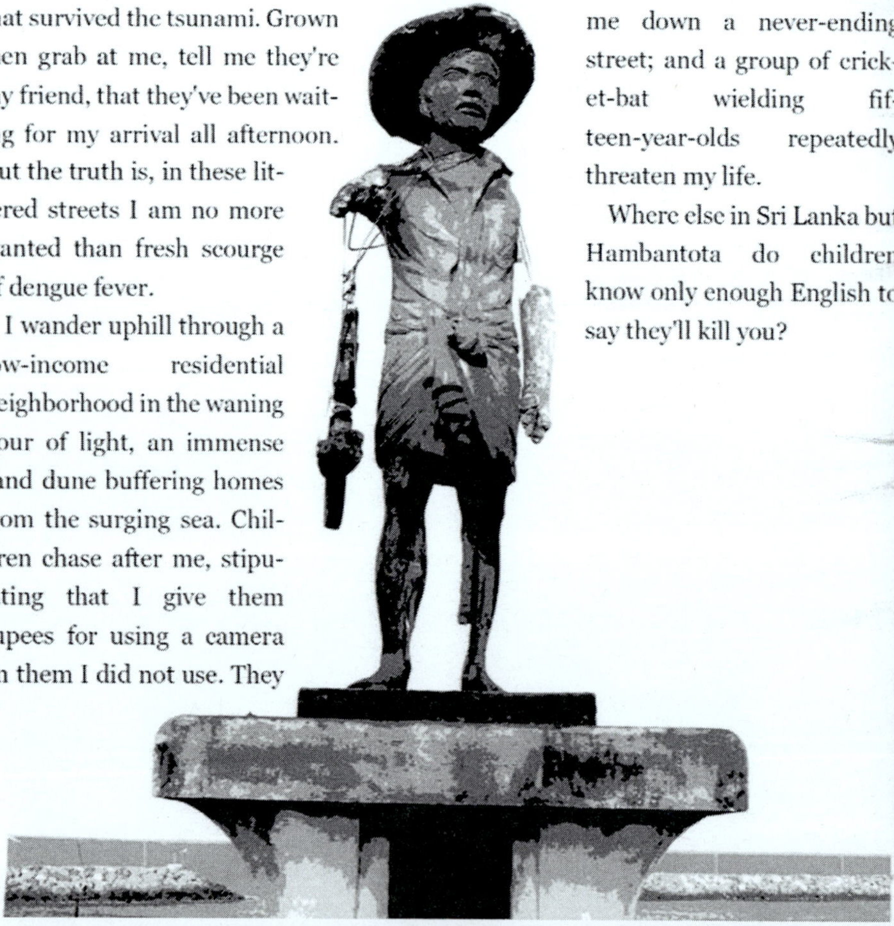

More hobo jaunts from www.Microcosm.Pub

Put more train on the brain at www.Microcosm.Pub

MAVERICK
VOLUME IV
MAVERICK
STRATFORD HOUSE
The Asian Journal of THOMAS MERTON
ROLI
AROUND INDIA IN 80 TRAINS
MONISHA RAJESH
Lotus Roli
CEYLON BEATEN TRACK
W.T. KEBLE
HOW TO SEE CEYLON
Bella Sidney Woolf
R. L. BROHIER
SEEING CEYLON
DISCOVERING CEYLON
R.L. BROHIER
TRAWICK
ENEMY LINES
WARFARE, CHILDHOOD, AND PLAY IN BATTICALOA
ADVENTURES IN STEAM
THE CAGE
THE FIGHT FOR SRI LANKA AND THE LAST DAYS OF THE TAMIL TIGERS
WEISS
BLP
WICKRAMASINGHE
SRI LANKA IN THE MODERN AGE
OXFORD
SINHALESE SELF-TAUGHT
WICKREMASINGHE
Bradt
Sri Lanka
ELEPHANT COMPLEX
JOHN GIMLETTE
A Comprehensive
ENRIQUE'S JOURNEY

SKILLS TO CHANGE YOUR LIFE AND THE WORLD
www.Microcosm.Pub
2752 N WILLIAMS AVE • PORTLAND, OR 97227

$7.95 U.S. / $9.99 CANADA

ISBN 978-1-62106-897-6
US$7.95
9 781621 068976
50795>